The Rescue, *Charles Belden.*

COW

DOUGLAS & McINTYRE   TORONTO/VANCOUVER

BOY

A KID'S ALBUM

By LINDA GRANFIELD

Acknowledgments

With thanks to Donna Livingstone of the Glenbow Museum, Alberta, for her expertise and eagerness to aid the cause. Special thanks to Richard Rattenbury, Historical Curator at the National Cowboy Hall of Fame in Oklahoma, who kindly read and critiqued the manuscript.

The following people have also given generously of their resources: the staff of The Baldwin Room, Metropolitan Toronto Reference Library; Elizabeth Benson; Elaine Bomberry, First Nations Talent Agency; the Calgary Stampede; Doug Chalmers and his daughter Jessica; Harvey Chan; Celia Chassles, Gary Goddard Management; Cinema Graphics, Toronto; Cinematheque Ontario; John Clayton, Paramount Pictures; Gary Clement; Colt's Manufacturing Company, Inc., Hartford, Connecticut; Mary Jane Culbert, Popular Culture, Toronto; Art and Rebecca de Vitalis, Ribbonhead Ranch House Gallery, Toronto; Donna Douglas, *TG Magazine,* Ontario; Elsa Dunsmoor, Biltmore Corporation, Guelph, Ontario; Tim Everett, Le Baron Outdoor Products; Pam Friendly, Premiere Arts Management; Tom Funicello, John B. Stetson Company, Mt. Kisco, New York; Andrew Gregg, producer, CBC; Camilla Gryski; Doug Harper; Mary Kiervin, CBC; Levi Strauss & Co.; Janet Lorenz, Center for Motion Picture Studies, Los Angeles, California; Pat Lowe and Greg Malak, Will Rogers Memorial, Claremore, Oklahoma; Stuart McLean; Marg Meikle, the "Answer Lady"; John Negru; Marilyn Peil, National Cowboy Hall of Fame and Western Heritage Center, Oklahoma City, Oklahoma; David Rae, CBC; Roy Rogers, Jr.; Marion and Michael Seary; Seth; Murray Sherman, CFTO-TV, Toronto; Ross Skoggard, *Toronto Star;* Hugh Standifer, Dallas; Texas Ranger Museum and Hall of Fame, Waco, Texas; the Tranah family; Deb and Ian Wallace, Toronto; the Western Folklife Center, Elko, Nevada; Dan Yamasaki; and lastly my supportive family, Cal, Devon and Brian Smiley, who stoked the campfire and settled for beans while I rode off in search of cowboys!

The lyrics of "Red River Valley" reprinted from *He Was Singin' This Song* by Jim Bob Tinsley. Orlando: University of Central Florida Press, 1981. Reprinted by permission of the publisher.

Illustration on page 5 by Brian Smiley.
Calligraphy on pages 45 and 47 by Elizabeth Benson.

A complete list of illustration credits appears on page 96.

The publisher gratefully acknowledges the assistance of the Canada Council.

Canadian Cataloguing in Publication Data

Granfield, Linda
    Cowboy : a kid's album

Includes index.
ISBN 1-55054-230-3

1. Cowboys—Juvenile literature. 2. West (U.S.)—Popular culture—Juvenile literature. I. Title.

F596.G73 1993   j636.2'01   C93-093949-2

Douglas & McIntyre Ltd.
585 Bloor Street West
Toronto, Ontario M6G 1K5

ILLUSTRATIONS BY SETH

Cover illustration by Harvey Chan
Design by Michael Solomon
Set in Alphatype Gamma and News Gothic, with display text in Adobe Birch and Adobe Willow, by Techni Process Lettering Limited, Toronto
Printed and bound in Hong Kong by Everbest Printing Co. Ltd.

For Brian Smiley,
my young buckaroo

CONTENTS

The Arizona Cowboy, *Frederic Remington, 1901, pastel and graphite on paper.*

Part I

THE HISTORICAL
COWBOY

The Birth of the Cowboy

Cowboy is actually a very old word. It has been traced to Ireland, where horsemen were called *cow-boys* almost two thousand years ago. During the American Revolution (1775–1783), the word *cowboy* became ugly. Some say it referred to thieves who stole cattle from the American colonists and sold them to the British army. Others claim it was used to describe people who were loyal to England and lured their enemies into ambush by jingling cowbells and pretending to be lost cattle.

By the the mid-1800s the word had returned to its original meaning—a hired man who works with cattle and performs many of his duties on horseback. Mexican cowboys were called *vaqueros*; later, American cowboys used the term *buckaroo*, which is how *vaquero* sounded to their ears.

Vaqueros in a Horse Corral, *James Walker.*

The era of the cowboy lasted only about twenty years, from about 1866 to 1886. During this time the demand for beef grew in the eastern United States, and men were needed to watch over the cattle as they grazed on the open range. More important, cowboys had to round up the cattle twice a year and herd them over the countryside to the railroad to be shipped east.

Ex-soldiers and runaway boys alike moved west looking for adventure and danger. For a while Eastern college men were also fascinated by the free, open life they had heard about. They flocked to the West, too, only to find they weren't up to the hard grind. A cowboy's job wasn't an easy one. He was often sinewy and strong, able to ride and rope well, able to withstand danger, heavy workloads, long days, and paltry pay. It's not surprising to learn that fewer than fifty thousand men rode the cattle trails during the cowboy's boom years.

Buenos días, amigo

During his working day, a cowboy spoke Spanish, whether he knew the language or not. Some, including Billy the Kid (see page 63), spoke Spanish fluently. But all cowboys were familiar with many Spanish terms (or words derived from the Spanish) that were first used by the Mexican vaqueros.

Here are just some of them:

amigo: Friend.

bronc: An untrained horse. From *bronco*, meaning "tough" or "wild."

calaboose: Jail. From *calabozo*, meaning "dungeon" or "prison cell."

chaparral: Dense thicket of thorny bush.

chaps: Abbreviation of *chaperejos*, meaning "leather leggings."

chili: A thick stew made of meat and peppers. From *chile*, meaning "red pepper."

cinch: From *cincha*, a wide strap to hold the saddle on a horse.

corral: Fenced yard for animals.

lariat: From *la reata*, meaning "the rope."

lasso: A rope with a running noose. From *lazo*, meaning "noose" or "slipknot."

pinto: A spotted horse, from *pinto*, meaning "spotted" or "speckled."

ranch: From *rancho*, meaning "camp," "small farm," "mess room."

remuda: Herd of spare saddle horses. From *remudar*, meaning "to exchange."

rodeo: Cattle roundup, or a demonstration of cowboys' skills. From *rodear*, meaning "to surround."

stampede: A sudden scattering of cattle or horses. From *estampida*, meaning "pounding" or "loud sound."

tapadero: A leather hood on the stirrup designed to protect the boot. From *tapadera*, meaning "cover" or "lid."

vaquero: A cowboy. From *vaca*, meaning "cow."

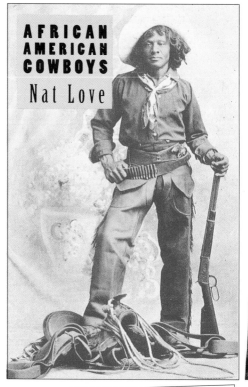

Nat Love
1854 – 1921

Nearly one out of seven cowboys was an African American freed from slavery by the Civil War. Nat Love was one of the most exciting African American cowboys. Born a slave in Tennessee, he had very little education but was good at breaking (taming) horses. Eventually he headed west and became a cowboy, winning roping and shooting competitions in rodeos. By the time Nat was in his thirties, cowboy life had worn him out (as it did many young men), and in 1890 he left his rough-and-tumble career to become a train porter. Readers loved his autobiography, published in 1907, which was filled with exaggerated stories of his life in the Old West.

John Ware
1845 – 1905

A cotton plantation was the first home of John Ware, another African American freed from slavery by the Civil War. Ware became a cowboy and drove Texas herds north to the territories of Wyoming and Montana. Some claimed he was the greatest bronco rider in the West, but he was equally talented with his pistol and his rope. After driving a large herd up to Calgary, Alberta, Ware decided to stay in Canada. He worked for Alberta cattle companies and later owned his own ranches.

Ware was admired for his good nature, his ability to leap into a saddle without using stirrups, and his constant courage—except when a snake crossed his path! He died when his horse stepped into a hole, threw him to the ground, and fell on top of him, and he was greatly mourned; his cabin in Alberta remains a tourist site.

Native Cowboys

The earliest North American cowboys came from the various Native tribes that lived throughout the United States Southwest. When the Spaniards came and settled in the 1500s, these able riders helped to manage the cattle herds.

As settlers moved farther west, they took over the traditional grounds of the Natives who made their home there. The United States set aside reservations, or certain areas for the Native tribes to live on. Part of this land was called Indian Territory (today the area is Oklahoma). Gradually settlers began to take over this land, too, moving the Natives onto smaller and smaller reservations.

Native cowboys found some freedom working on the cattle drives, where their skills in breaking wild horses, handling cattle, and surviving the tough conditions of the Western plains were invaluable. A cowboy who spoke a Native language would have been welcomed by a trail boss who had to lead his herds through Indian Territory. By law, Native Americans could charge a toll of one dollar per head of cattle driven across their land, and there could be an additional charge of one cow from each herd as payment for the grass the cattle ate as they crossed the reservation. A Native cowboy might have been just the negotiator needed by a worried trail boss.

Women

Most women who lived on the American frontier worked as long and hard as men, under equally tough conditions. But in those days women were still expected to dress and behave like "proper" gentlewomen. During the late 1800s, the sight of a woman riding astride a horse caused a scandal. A real lady rode a horse only on a sidesaddle, and that was no way to cover rough cattle territory. The long, full skirts worn by women were yet another nuisance of the times.

Women were expected to spend their energy tending homes for their families, not tending cattle out on the range. Still, some women did get a taste of cowboy life in the early trail days. Sometimes ranchers' wives managed the family cattle business when their husbands were away, or after the men had died. Unmarried daughters sometimes became "cowwomen" and ranchers in their own right. A few young women became cowhands or traveled as cowgirls with the Wild West shows (see page 69). Others went on to become champion athletes in rodeos (see page 86).

WOMEN OF THE WILD WEST

CALAMITY JANE

Calamity Jane
(Martha Jane Canary)
1848? – 1903

Martha Jane Canary was born in Missouri and moved west with her family while she was in her teens. She dressed in men's clothes, which she found more comfortable and practical for frontier life, but this raised eyebrows wherever she traveled. Legend has it that she got her nickname when she announced that calamity would befall anyone who opposed her. Calamity Jane became known as the Heroine of Whoop-Up, because she was a rough-and-ready character and was well known in all the saloons. It was said that she worked as a mule-driver, a railroad laborer and an army scout. Eventually she traveled with a Wild West show and became the heroine of many novels and plays.

WOMEN OF THE WILD WEST

ALICE GREENOUGH

Alice Greenough
1902 –

Alice Greenough's father headed west when he was a teenager. He ended up in Montana, where he met Calamity Jane. She took care of him, and in return he cut and sold wood to earn the money that she spent in the local saloon.

Five of the eight Greenough children competed in rodeos and became known as the Riding Greenoughs. Alice and her sister Marge were two of the great women bronc riders in the 1930s (see page 87). Alice won many rodeo titles and traveled around the world, but she still found time to train horses and produce her own rodeo shows. She also acted in Hollywood westerns and later worked on television shows; she even had a job as a stunt driver on the *Little House on the Prairie* series. Alice, Marge, and one of their brothers were inducted into the National Cowboy Hall of Fame in 1983.

13

Home Sweet Home

Many men spent most of their cowboy lives traveling from one place to another looking for jobs. Ranch owners relied on this short-term labor force to get the work done around their homes and out on the open prairies. Cowboys received "thirty and found"—thirty dollars a month plus meals and lodging—to work on the property.

Ranches came in all sizes. The acreage included an outside spring for water, a house for the owner and his family, and a number of outbuildings. Early ranch buildings were made of sod or logs, but if the ranch owner later enjoyed high profits from selling his cattle, his family lived in relative splendor, with lace curtains, fine furniture, china plates, and silver. The hired hands, however, lived more frugal lives in the bunkhouse.

Some ranches were large enough to have a cookhouse. This was a separate building just for cooking and eating. Long tables filled the rooms. Outside the bunkhouse there would be a blacksmith shop to provide shoes for the horses and tools, as well as stables and a corral for the horses. The corral was circular so the horses couldn't injure themselves by crowding into sharp corners.

Surrounding the ranch were huge stretches of unfenced prairies. Cattle from several ranches might wander freely over this open range until they were gathered together by the cowboys during the spring and fall roundups.

Often the names of ranches related to the chosen brand or mark of the ranch owner (see page 42). For example, the JA Ranch was owned by John Adair, and his brand looked like the two letters. The Four Sixes Ranch in Texas was known by its 6666 brand.

Other ranch names had nothing to do with their brands. The Matador Ranch had a flying-V brand. Many names became famous. The 101 Ranch in Oklahoma was known worldwide after the ranch organized a traveling western show featuring Bill Pickett (see page 89).

A foreman was in charge of the cowboys, and he lived with about ten of them in the bunkhouse. The building had a kitchen and dining area at one end, a potbellied stove in the middle, and a line of beds (bunks) at the other end. On the Northern ranches, the bunkhouse walls were often lined with layers of newspaper to keep out the cold winds. The cowboys tacked up pictures of their relatives and popular actresses to decorate the dark room, which was usually lit by oil lamps. A few pegs on the wall above the bed served as a man's "closet." A trunk at the foot of the bed might hold his few possessions.

Some cowboys remembered bunkhouses as being vile-smelling from all the sweating, unwashed men inside. At roundup time, extra cowboys were hired to help out, and they added to the bunkhouse confusion. Others commented on the terrible language you would hear. Still others complained about the dull life in the bunkhouse. Gambling was not allowed. Instead, games of checkers or dominoes kept the idle cowboys entertained until the next cattle drive and the few days they would enjoy in the cities spending their hard-earned cash. Books were not common around a bunkhouse, because many cowboys couldn't read.

NO 22 THE CO

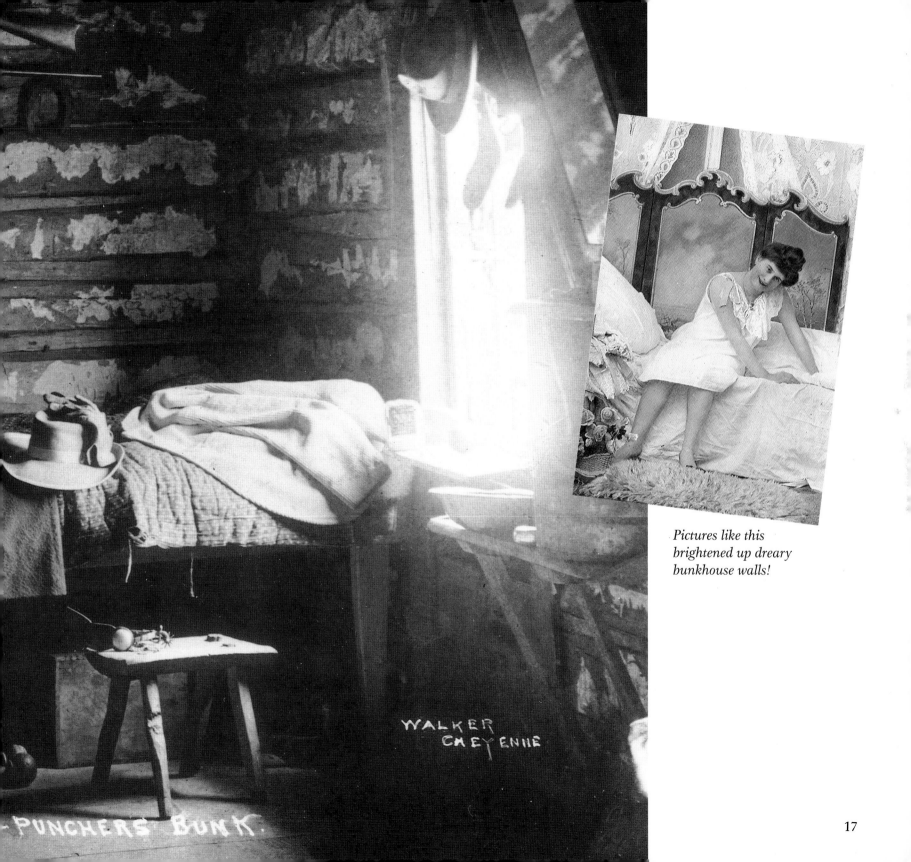

WALKER
CHEYENNE

PUNCHERS' BUNK.

*Pictures like this
brightened up dreary
bunkhouse walls!*

"Git along, little dogies!"

The longhorn beef cattle that cowboys were paid to move from place to place had not always been in North America. They were brought to the continent by the Spanish in the 1520s, and proved ideal for the rugged, dry conditions of Mexico and the American Southwest. Longhorns were a strong breed that needed little more than water and grass. Many of these original longhorn cattle were turned loose, and their descendants were the longhorns of the cowboys' heyday.

There were disadvantages to owning longhorns. True to their name, the cattle had very long pointed horns, from tip to tip about one-and-a-half times as long as a man. The horns became weapons when the unpredictable animals decided to attack a man or other animals. This half-wild breed also had a bad temper and couldn't be handled like tamer breeds. Nevertheless, the longhorns were valuable property.

Early settlers raised cattle to provide their own families with meat, or to sell in small quantities in nearby towns. Leather was made out of cattle hides. Horns and hooves were used to make buckles, buttons, and ornaments, and tallow (fat) was melted to make candles and soap, but there was not a large market for beef. People ate more pork.

The Civil War changed all that. After the war began in 1861, a man named Philip Armour began selling beef to the army. His business was such a success that he opened a meat-packing plant in Chicago in 1870. Easterners decided they liked the taste of beef and wanted more of it. The longhorns became a beef bonanza. Before the war, Texas cattle sold in the North for about three dollars a head. By 1866, the price was up to forty dollars a head. This meant plenty of work for the cowboys and plenty of money for the ranchers. Some ranchers became so rich and powerful that they were said to run "cattle empires."

The longhorn cows were gradually bred with Hereford bulls from England. The result was the whiteface cow, an animal that brought in more money than a longhorn because it was heavier and meatier.

Before the days of cattle ranching, huge herds of buffalo roamed over the North American plains. Native people hunted them for food and clothing. But with the settling of the West, the buffalo quickly disappeared. By the late 1870s, the buffalo was nearly extinct, leaving plenty of grassland for the growing numbers of grazing cattle and the ranchers. Some ranches covered nearly half a million acres. By 1885, almost half the land in the United States was devoted to raising cattle for the beef industry.

A Texas Long Horn Steer, Width of Horns 9 Feet.

Till the cows come home...

Here are some of the other names used for cattle:

bull: The male of the breed.
calf: A young cow or bull.
cow: The female of the breed. On a ranch sometimes all cattle are called cows, regardless of their sex.
dogie: A motherless calf, or any young or stray calf.

heifer: A young cow that has not had a calf.
steer: A young male raised for beef.

…and two names a cowboy might hear:

greenhorn: Originally, this meant a young animal with immature horns. Later, the name referred to an inexperienced newcomer on a ranch.
tenderfoot: Another name for a cowboy who is new to the job, the word originally described Eastern cattle that were shipped west for breeding.

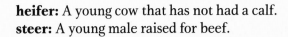

.ches

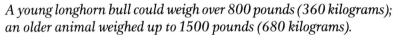

A young longhorn bull could weigh over 800 pounds (360 kilograms); an older animal weighed up to 1500 pounds (680 kilograms).

Lead steers were very important to a rancher. A good animal kept the cattle moving and led them into the railyard pens. Old Blue, owned by Charles Goodnight (1836–1929), was a famous lead steer that trekked 250 miles (400 kilometers) from the Texas Panhandle to Dodge City, Kansas, sometimes twice a year for eight years.

Goodnight attached a bell to Blue's tail, and its sound set the pace for the rest of the cattle. At night, a cowboy filled the bell with grass to muffle the clapper—a sudden clanging could start a stampede. After the cattle were herded into the railway cars, Old Blue waited with the remuda while the cowboys stayed in Dodge City. Then it was time to walk back to the ranch, until the next drive to the cow town.

Old Blue was a true-life animal hero, and he lived to be twenty years old.

The Cowboy's Companion

It's hard to imagine a cowboy without a horse close by. His way of life depended on the animal that carried him through the day's work. At night, his horse was always nearby, ready for any emergency, such as a stampede of cattle spooked by a sudden storm, or a midnight attack by cattle rustlers.

A good cow pony was a prized possession. Descendants of the horses brought to North America by the Spaniards had been allowed to run free, and eventually these hardy animals became mustangs, the wild horses of the prairies.

But mustangs had to be captured and broken before they could become good cow ponies. And breaking the wild horses was a dangerous job. After saddling the horse, a cowboy had to mount it and stay on while the horse tried to buck the man off its back. Bronco-busters were cowboys who only broke horses. They moved from ranch to ranch, and were paid a fee for each horse. After many attempts and plenty of bruises, the horse was tame enough to be taught cow-pony skills.

A cowboy might own his own horse, but most of the horses he worked with were ranch property. Many ranches supplied up to six horses per cowboy, and the cowboy's choice of horse depended on the chores that had to be done. Riding the line (patrolling the farthest reaches of the ranch) was good training for a newly broken horse. If the horse was a good swimmer, he'd be used to urge the cattle across a river during the drive.

Night horses were skilled at finding their way in the dark without stumbling into dangerous prairie-dog holes that could cripple the horse and injure the rider.

The most trained horse was the highly prized cutting horse, used to cut, or separate, the unbranded calves from their mothers during the roundup. This tough and agile horse was trained to respond to the rider's slightest touch while the man tried to rope a calf. Then the horse had to stand strong when the calf tried to pull away.

A cowboy cared well for his horses, because his work depended on them. (During a roundup, a cowboy used three or four horses a day.) Some cowboys fed their horses breakfast before they ate their own. Others refused to allow anyone else to ride their assigned cow ponies.

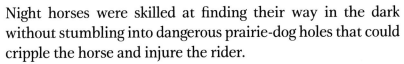

Horses of Another Name

bronc/bronco: A rough, wild horse.

broomtail: A range horse with a straggly tail.

cayuse: A small horse, especially an Indian (Cayuse) pony.

outlaw: A horse that cannot be broken.

pinto: A "painted," or spotted, horse.

quarter horse: A small animal that can run quickly for short distances. It is descended from a breed trained to run quarter-mile races in the East.

sorrel: A reddish-brown horse.

sun fisher: A bucking bronc.

Tall in
the Saddle

The cowboy with a healthy, trained horse and a well-made saddle could ride fifteen hours in a day… and the horse could still go on. That's because a good saddle placed the rider's weight on the horse's shoulders, rather than on its spine.

Saddles cost anywhere from one month's to ten months' salary (thirty to three hundred dollars), but the price was worth paying. A good saddle could last almost thirty years. It was such an important item to a cowboy that he even used it as a pillow at night. The expression *he's sold his saddle* meant the man had retired from cowboy life.

There were many styles of saddles, but the basic construction remained the same. The foundation was built of wood and metal, to take the stress of riding and roping, and it was covered with layers of rawhide and leather. The leather often had beautiful carved and raised decorations that actually helped hold the rider in the seat. The finished saddle could weigh up to forty pounds (eighteen kilograms).

The horn on the front of the saddle was used to hold one end of the lasso when the cowboy was roping. Long leather flaps on each side, called *fenders*, protected the rider's legs from horse sweat, and thongs or leather strips along the back were used to tie on extra equipment, such as overcoats or saddlebags.

A cowboy's stirrups were longer than those on other kinds of saddles. The longer length made it easier for him to get in and out of the saddle quickly, and let the cowboy ride with his legs hanging almost straight down. This position was handy when riding down steep slopes; then the cowboy was almost standing straight up in the broad stirrups. Some cowboys liked to add a wedge-shaped piece of tough leather called a *tapadero* to the stirrup. This "tap," or hood, protected the rider's foot from brush and thorns.

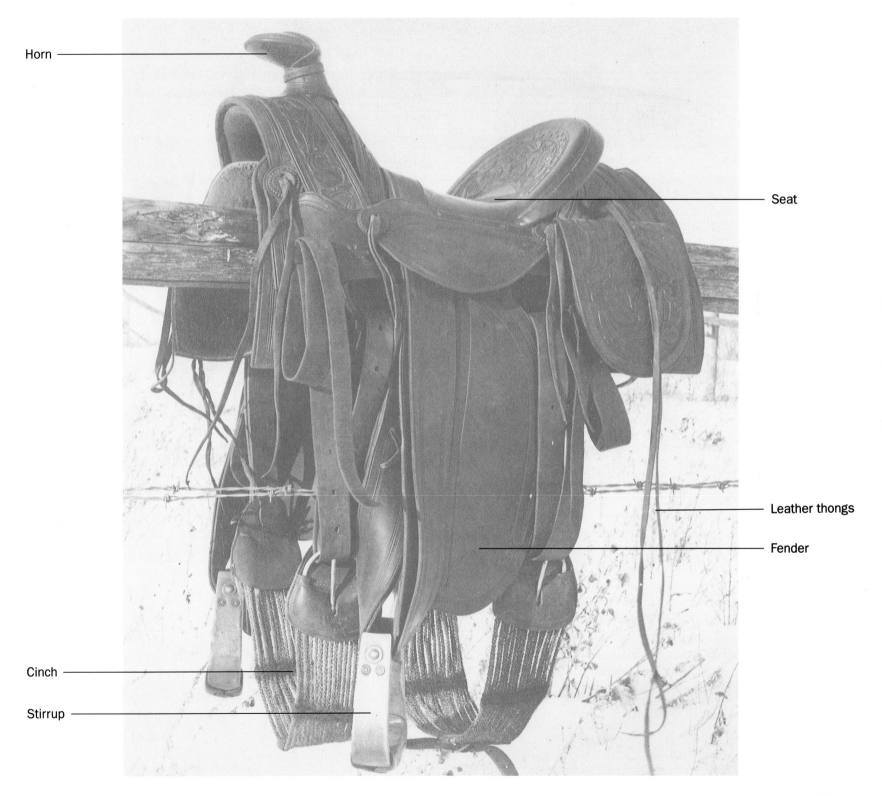

Horn

Seat

Leather thongs

Fender

Cinch

Stirrup

Ropes

Braiding Skills

Cowboys were excellent braiders. They braided leather strips to make everything from lariats, quirts (riding whips), and hatbands, to hobbles (to tie a horse's legs together to stop it from straying). Braiding added strength, and the thongs could be used to lash together corrals and fences when wire and staples were not available. Thongs were even used to make seats and backs for the bunkhouse chairs.

Horsehair was also a popular material for handiwork by cowboys. After the spring roundup, the tangled tails of the cow ponies were combed, and the long, loose hairs were bundled into sacks and saved. Then, during the long winter evenings in the bunkhouse, the cowboys twisted and braided the hair to make reins, hatbands, and belts. Fancy horsehair tassels decorated many products, including horsehair saddle blankets that were woven from different colors of hair (mainly gray and black) to make patterns.

A Mix Up, Charles M. Russell, 1910, oil on canvas.

Without ropes, a cowboy couldn't do his job. He needed ropes to lasso cattle, hold his horses, help pull the chuck wagon across muddy stretches, and tie his equipment in place.

The lariat (from the Spanish *la reata,* meaning "rope") was first used by the vaqueros, who braided rawhide and attached one braided length to another until the lariat reached about sixty feet (eighteen meters)—long enough to rope a calf or steer. The rawhide lariat was about as thick as a pencil. It formed a large loop when one end was passed through the honda, or eyelet, which was made of metal or cow horn. The honda allowed the rope to slide so that the loop could easily become larger or smaller.

Later, cowboys made their lariats or lassos from twisted grass. By the 1890s, many used ropes made from hemp, similar to the lines used on sailing ships. These new lariats could be knotted to form the honda, and they were long enough to be dallied (one end wrapped around the saddle horn after the steer was roped).

A new lariat was stiff. Some cowboys made it more pliable by tying one end to the saddle horn, and dragging the full length of the lariat on the ground for several days.

To toss the lariat, a cowboy held the main line and the loop in his throwing hand. In his other hand, he held the remaining coils of the lariat, so that he could "pay out" (let out) extra rope as he needed it. This same hand had to hold the reins and steer the horse. No wonder cowboys spent a great deal of their spare time practicing their rope skills!

The Cowboy's Uniform

Old photographs show cowboys in their clean "best" clothes, gazing into the camera with their hands on their hips and their guns ready to blaze for the folks back home. But a cowboy's job was tough, and his clothing had to be sensible and simple.

A cowboy didn't own much more than the clothes on his back. There was little storage space in the bunkhouse and few, if any, laundry days on a cattle drive to keep his clothes in good shape. Whatever he called his best clothes were saved for the few dances or socials in town—and those photographers' studios!

......3048. A Real Live Cowboy.

The cowboy on the left has dressed up to pose in a photographer's studio, but a "real live cowboy" looked a little more rugged. The above photograph is a stereograph. Each picture is taken at a slightly different angle. Viewed together through a stereoscope, the combined images look like a three-dimensional picture.

The Hat

Every cowboy wore a hat, and it was one of his most treasured possessions. A cowboy could wear his hat indoors while he ate or danced, and was still said to have good manners, since everyone knew how important his hat was to him. Some cowboys even wore their hats to bed. Usually sweat-stained and well-worn, the cowboy's hat was practical as well as being a symbol of his way of life.

The broad-brimmed hat evolved from the large sombrero worn by the Mexican vaqueros. Made of black, gray, or brown felt, the hat cost a cowboy between three and fifteen dollars. The brim protected the scalp and neck from the scorching sun of the prairies, and kept rain and hail off the face. In the winter, the brim could be tied down like flaps to make "earmuffs." The crown of the hat could be used as a bucket to hold water for a man or horse to drink, or to carry feed to the animal. A hat was also used to fan the flames of a fading campfire, or swat flying insects.

In the 1870s the high-crowned creation of hatter J.B. Stetson became very popular, and many cowboy hats were called Stetsons, whether they were made by J.B. or not. But different areas of the West had different styles, and cowboys soon found dozens of ways to personalize their hats. Some put unusual creases in the crown. Others circled the crown with a belt of leather or silver, or woven bands. A leather chin strap, possibly braided by the cowboy himself, kept the valuable hat from blowing off and away.

the last drop from his STETSON

29

The Neckerchief

The neckerchief was a simple square of cheap cotton, but it had plenty of uses. Folded in a triangle to tie at the front or back, it hung loosely around the neck so that it could be pulled over the face quickly. It served as a breathing mask to keep out trail dust, and it could be dampened and sucked on to relieve thirst under the blazing sun. It could become a tourniquet in case of rattlesnake bites, and it protected the neck from sunburn. The neckerchief bandaged wounds and filtered dirt out of drinking water. It wiped a sweaty brow, a dripping nose, or a tearful eye.

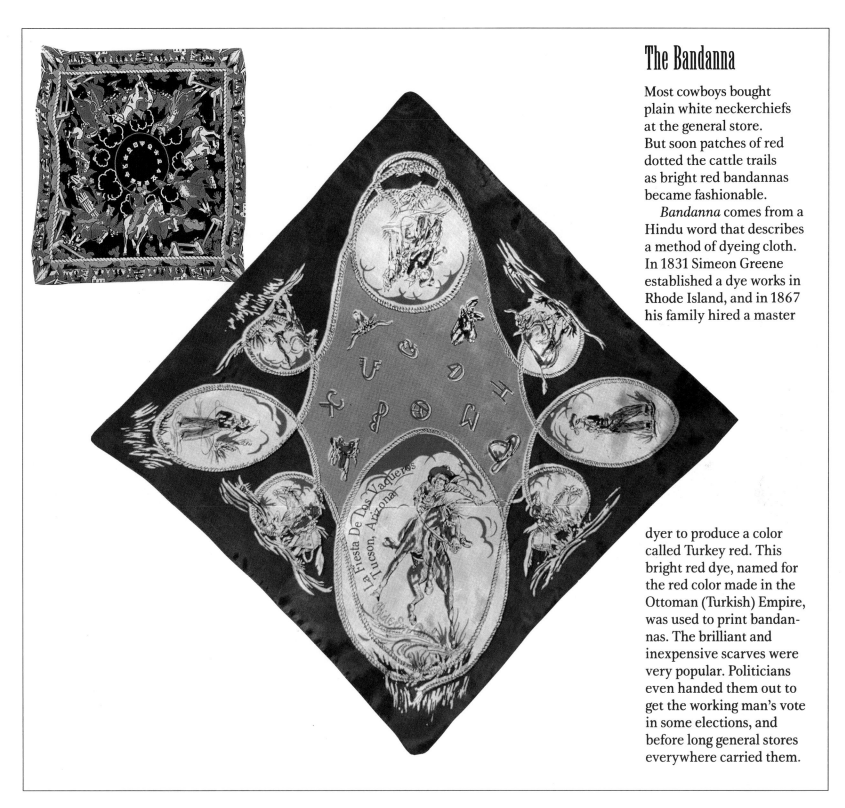

The Bandanna

Most cowboys bought plain white neckerchiefs at the general store. But soon patches of red dotted the cattle trails as bright red bandannas became fashionable.

Bandanna comes from a Hindu word that describes a method of dyeing cloth. In 1831 Simeon Greene established a dye works in Rhode Island, and in 1867 his family hired a master dyer to produce a color called Turkey red. This bright red dye, named for the red color made in the Ottoman (Turkish) Empire, was used to print bandannas. The brilliant and inexpensive scarves were very popular. Politicians even handed them out to get the working man's vote in some elections, and before long general stores everywhere carried them.

Under It All

A cowboy usually wore long johns, or one-piece underwear, beneath his work clothing. Long johns covered the body from neck to ankle, and had a long, buttoned opening down the front. A cowboy wore his long johns day and night, unless it was extremely hot. Then he went without this extra layer of warm, itchy, and maybe bug-ridden clothing.

This collarless shirt was fancier than those worn by most working cowboys. The rigid leather cuffs protected the wrists and lower arms from rope burns.

The Shirt

A look at old photographs shows how worn-out a working cowboy's shirt could become on the trail. In the summer, the collarless shirts were made of cotton. Winter versions were made of wool. Some shirts had checked or striped patterns, but generally they looked very drab. Sometimes there was a bib panel in front, where a double layer of cloth added extra protection for the chest during cold weather. Fancy embroidery and piping appeared on yokes and cuffs when cowboys with Wild West shows started to wear fancier duds for their performances.

The Vest

Cowboys spent most of their waking hours in the saddle, and it's difficult to reach into trouser pockets when you're astride a moving horse. So a cowboy often wore a vest with deep pockets to carry any small items he might need during the day—maybe a knife, or a little poke (buckskin purse) to carry a bit of money. Vest pockets might also hold a pouch of tobacco, a pencil, or a branding book (see page 42). Cowboys seldom carried pocket watches, because they were expensive and easily broken out on the trail. Besides, a person who worked outdoors could tell the time simply by watching the sun and the stars. If he did have a watch, a cowboy might attach it to the inside of his pocket with a chain that he'd braided with hair plucked from the tails of his trail mounts.

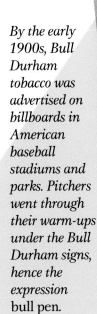

By the early 1900s, Bull Durham tobacco was advertised on billboards in American baseball stadiums and parks. Pitchers went through their warm-ups under the Bull Durham signs, hence the expression bull pen.

Bull Durham

Tobacco was an important item in many cowboys' vest pockets. Some men liked to take snuff, crushed tobacco that they sniffed up through the nose. Others enjoyed chewing on a lump of tobacco. Both snuff and chewing tobacco had two advantages. They freed up the cowboy's hands for his work, and they didn't require a match —a dangerous item on a dry prairie.

But other cowboys carried small bags of Bull Durham tobacco, which they rolled into cigarettes. The brand became popular with the roll-your-own cowboys because of the bag's drawstring top. A smoker could easily and quickly close the bag by pulling the drawstring with his teeth, again leaving a hand free to hold the reins or lariat.

Developed in the East, the Bull Durham brand was taken west by settlers. Some felt that sharing a Bull Durham cigarette with a stranger on the trail was a gesture of friendship, and that to refuse a "Bull" was as bad as an insult. The Bull was also used as a western land measure. The buyer and seller lit cigarettes and walked along the proposed border of land. The point where they finished smoking the cigarettes marked the length of land in the arrangement.

Pants and Chaps

Until denim came into use, woolen pants were worn no matter what the weather, and they soon became shapeless and patched. Some pants were strengthened with buckskin pieces sewn to the seat and inner thigh areas. Suspenders were not worn, because they rubbed against the shoulders and restricted a cowboy's arm movements. And a belt was never part of the cowboy's "uniform." Pants were bought to fit tightly around the waist, because belts could be dangerous. If a bucking horse kicked a cowboy in the stomach while he was wearing a tightly buckled belt, the man could be seriously injured.

Chaps provided extra leg protection. Chaps (pronounced *shaps*) is short for the Spanish word *chaperejos*, meaning "leather breeches." The seatless leather pants kept the woolen pants underneath from being ripped by the thick scrub brush and cactus found on the range. They protected the cowboy's legs from long cattle horns and rough fences; they also prevented

rope burns and horse nibbles. Some riders dampened the inside of the chaps to help them get a tighter leg grip on the horse, but this practice was frowned upon by experienced riders.

Wide chaps, or batwings, protected the flanks of the horse as well, and a man could wrap them on without taking off his boots and spurs. Other styles were narrow and hugged the rider's legs. Texans called their chaps *leggins* or *shotguns*. Chaps that came down only to the knee were called *chinks*.

Cowboys who worked in colder areas, like Montana and Wyoming, often wore "hair pants"—goat-hair chaps that kept their legs warm. Unfortunately, when the hair-covered pants got wet, they became soggy and heavy and, as one cowboy said, "sometimes smellin' stronger 'n a wolf's den."

Cowboys usually wore their chaps only when they were on horseback on the range, but some wore them in town, too.

From the Old West...to you

Cowboys needed sturdy clothing that could take the daily wear and tear of the range. In 1850, during the California Gold Rush, a young German immigrant named Levi Strauss came to San Francisco to sell canvas tents and wagon covers. But he soon learned that the miners really wanted work pants that would last. The enterprising Strauss joined forces with a tailor. They produced "waist overalls," the first pair of work pants, and soon they were in the clothing business.

In the 1870s, Levi Strauss and his partner were granted a patent for the copper fasteners that reinforced the pockets and seams of their pants. Miners could stuff the pockets full of rocks and still the pants wouldn't tear.

Cowboys appreciated the heavy-duty work pants, too. They quickly replaced their baggy worn-out woolen pants with Levis. Soon the canvas material was replaced by a tough cotton indigo-blue fabric called *denim*. That cloth has been used ever since to produce the pants that are still worn by cowboys but also bought by fashion models, nobility... and you.

The Boots

The cowboy's footwear was an important and very expensive item. In the 1880s, a pair of boots cost between ten and twenty-five dollars, a high price for a man who made about thirty dollars for one month's work. It's no wonder many a man "slept with his boots on."

Well-made boots were needed to brace a rider in his saddle. Early models had flat heels, but in the late 1860s the "cowboy boot" appeared. The high heels helped keep the foot from slipping out of the stirrups, kept the spurs clear of the ground, and added some extra inches to a vain cowboy's height. The boot also had a reinforced arch and narrow toes that helped the cowboy get into the stirrups quickly—and get out safely if he was thrown by a horse.

Cowboy boots were made for riding, not for walking. The soles were constructed of thin leather so that the rider could feel the stirrup. The tall boots protected the lower legs from rain, and fit snugly at the top to keep out pebbles and twigs. Some cowboys claimed the tighter the boot, the better it was, and they often had the sore feet and limps to show for their vanity.

Later boot styles included "mule ears" with long leather straps that made the boots easier to pull on. By the end of the cowboy's heyday, "fancy" boots were decorated with lots of stitching and had scalloped tops.

Spurs were practical items for the job, and they attracted attention on the wooden sidewalks and floors of cow towns. The heel band fit over the back of the boot, and a strap fastened across the front. A chain kept the spur from sliding up the boot. Some had "jinglebobs," or danglers, to create more noise when a cowboy strutted about.

The business part of the spur was the rowel, a small, blunt-spiked wheel that was used to prick a horse lightly to urge it to go faster or to help the cowboy hang onto a bucking bronco.

The rowel was not intended to injure the horse. In fact, sharp rowels were often filed down for the safety of both the horse and its rider. It was said that rowel scars on a horse were the sign of a poor horseman.

The work spur was plain. But when it came time to impress, a cowboy might have a pair of fancy silver spurs that had never seen the mud of a corral. These special items were often etched with scroll designs and flower patterns on the heel band and rowel.

Foul-weather protection: A cowboy keeps his slicker handily tied behind his saddle.

Extras

Other pieces of the cowboy's wardrobe provided extra warmth and protection, both on the ranch and on the drive. He might have a lined canvas overcoat with long sections (skirts) to cover his knees and protect his legs from thorns. Often the outside was painted yellow—the traditional color of rain slickers. Northern cowboys needed fur-lined coats, which were often supplied by the rancher because they were so expensive.

Tough buckskin gloves (gauntlets) were worn in the winter and when a cowboy was roping. The leather prevented rope burns and blisters. Northern cowboys used warm woolen mittens in the winter, when they climbed into the high hills looking for strays.

Cowboyspeak

A cowboy's language was a colorful mix of words and expressions. The language reflected the many cultures found in any group of cowmen: Mexican, French, British, Jewish, Native, Canadian Métis and African American. Writers in the 1920s collected some of the cowboy vocabulary. Imaginative novelists made up other words as they wrote their books, and claimed the lingo was "gen-u-ine." What we call *cowboyspeak* is a blend of documented and invented words and expressions, kept alive and embroidered in today's western movies and books.

Here's a typical conversation between a couple of cowhands, sitting around a campfire as they might have done over one hundred years ago.

Translation:

A. Well, Slim, I'm getting a little fed up. I'm sick of eating beans every day. Pass the coffee, will you?

B. I agree with you, buddy. I'd like some canned fruit on the next drive. Some milk would taste pretty good, too.

Did you hear Dutch last night? He wouldn't stop talking about his firearms. I plan to stick a prairie dog in his bunk the next time he does that. I was tired, and he kept going on about them.

A. As for me, I'm going to roll a cigarette and forget all about it. That newcomer will learn, pal. He'll walk into the bunkhouse and find his mail-order catalogue missing. If his holsters are missing, too, he'll be pretty scared.

B. Roll me a cigarette, will you? It's time to get to work. Boy, will I be happy when this drive is over!

39

Part II

ROUNDUP

Cutting Out a Steer,
Frederic Remington, 1888,
oil on academy board.

The Daily Grind

Long ago there were no fences to mark ranch boundaries, and cattle ran freely on the huge range. There was plenty of grass and water, so everybody's cattle grazed together. While the cattle ate and gained weight on the open prairie, the cowboys checked on them regularly. The rest of the time the cowboys stayed on the ranch, repairing their equipment and doing other odd jobs.

In the spring and fall, however, a cowboy left behind his boring ranch chores and joined the roundup. During a roundup, cattle were collected from the range, sorted, counted, and branded. For several weeks, cowboys from area ranches worked

together and rode out over hundreds of miles to gather in all the longhorns. The men were divided into squads; each squad was responsible for the strays in one area of the range.

The cowboys worked from morning until night. After breakfast, fresh horses were taken from the remuda (the herd of spare horses), which was often kept in a rope corral near the chuck wagon. The wrangler in charge of the remuda was usually a "student cowboy," a youth learning how to be a cowpuncher. After the cowboys saddled their morning horses and rode into the range, the cook and the wrangler moved the chuck wagon and the remuda to a new roundup ground several miles away. The new spot became the center for the day's activities.

Mornings were spent finding and gathering the cattle. The cowboys stopped for a hot meal at noon. In the afternoons, the cattle were counted and sorted according to their markings or brands, which showed who they belonged to. Sick or weak animals were removed from the group, and new calves were branded. Other animals were chosen for the herd that would be driven to market.

Branding

Get Along Little Dogie   TX15

Branding Cattle in Corral, Western Canada.

Once the cattle were rounded up, the calves that had been born since the previous roundup had to be branded. Brands, or marks, permanently identified an animal as belonging to a certain rancher. Branding irons have been used since the days of the Egyptians, and Spanish herdsmen brought the tradition to North America. Before long, registry books throughout the West listed all the ranchers' brands and the owners' names and addresses. Some cowboys claimed they knew thousands of brand marks, and many a trail boss carried a pocket-size branding book in his vest for quick reference during roundups and cattle drives.

New calves always stayed close to their mothers, so that a young animal's owner was determined by the brand on the cow. But first the cowboys and cutting horses (see page 21) had to separate the calves from their mothers. The bellowing calf was roped and dragged to a branding fire, often while its angry mother tried to attack the horse and its rider.

At the fire, two cowboys called *flankers* grabbed the calf,

flipped it onto its side and pinned it to the ground. Quickly, the ironman (brander) pressed a red-hot branding iron on the calf's hip, neck, jaw, or other spot picked by the owner. The scar from the burn would leave a permanent mark. Once the branding was done, the cows and their calves "mothered up" again and returned to the herd.

It took about four seconds to brand a calf, and a skilled crew could handle more than one hundred animals in an hour. Sometimes other identifying marks were made as well. Notches might be cut in the calf's ear, or on the skin under its neck. One marking, the "jinglebob," involved cutting the ear so that the two halves hung down beside the calf's neck.

Western newspapers regularly printed lists of lost-and-found cattle. Stray cattle could wander hundreds of miles away from their ranches. An honest rancher and cowboy always returned any strays to their rightful owners, and they expected the same treatment in return.

Maverick

A maverick is an unbranded calf. The word comes from Colonel Samuel Maverick, a Texas pioneer who decided not to brand his cattle. The colonel claimed that because all the other ranchers branded their animals, everyone would know that any unbranded cattle belonged to him. In time, new calves or any other unbranded strays came to be called mavericks.

Today, people who refuse to do the same thing as everyone else are also called mavericks.

THE BIG FOUR

Brand Book

CONTAINING

Nearly all the Brands West of the 100th Meridian to the Foot Hills on all Four Rivers: Arkansas, Cimarron, Beaver, and Canadian Rivers and their Tributaries, Covering the Parts of Five States: Kansas, Colorado, Oklahoma Territory, Texas and New Mexico.

FOR THE SPRING WORK OF 1897.

These Brands were all Gathered New in the Year 1896.

EAR-MARK.

Left   Right

Published by C. V. SHEPLER, 614 Charlotte St., KANSAS CITY, MO.

Press of HUDSON-KIMBERLY PUB. CO.

The Long Drive

No 56 " General View of Round U...

The Chisholm Trail ——

Once the cattle had been rounded up and were ready to be sold, ranchers had to get the animals to the Northern railroads, where they were sent by train to the East. By the late 1860s, the railroad stretched into Kansas, and towns like Abilene and Dodge City sprang up at the railheads (ends of the tracks). Cattle drives were the only way to get the herds from southern Texas to the nearest rail yards. Over time, millions of hooves wore trails up to a quarter of a mile wide through the dusty Texas soil. Between 1866 and 1886, about five million cattle traveled the trails to market.

The long, exhausting drives were powerful lessons in life for a young man who wanted to become a full-fledged cowboy. These letters from one imaginary young cowboy to his sweetheart back east give us a picture of life on the trail.

The cattle ranchers used a number of trails, but the most famous was the Chisholm Trail, named for Jesse Chisholm (1806–1868), an early Native trader who first marked this route through Indian Territory (see page 12) to Kansas. Cowboys liked the route because it was flat and open, with no hills or wooded areas where coyotes or rustlers could hide. The trail and its branches stretched from southern Texas, crossed at least seven rivers, and led to Dodge City, Abilene, and Ellsworth, Kansas.

On the Trail

June, 1872

Dear Jennie,
I hope this letter finds you well and prospering. There is plenty to tell you about my days and nights. Since I've come to Texas I have found ranch work and am often weary.

We are pushing nearly three thousand cattle to Abilene, Kansas, and will travel the Chisholm Trail for hundreds of miles—and eight weeks, I am told. There are about a dozen of us on this drive. Our days are long and I'm afraid my time to write will be short, but I will try to write often.

The first few days on the trail were the most difficult, as the cattle were hard to control so close to home. But now we travel about fifteen miles a day. Our herd stretches in a dusty line as far as the eye can see, and we must keep the animals moving slow and steady. If the cattle smell water they get very excited, and want to run fast to taste it. But if they go too fast, they lose weight and bring in less money at the market.

Oh, Jennie, we are just a few days on the trail and I long for a meal at your table, with white cloths and glasses that shine! The chuck is beans, beef, and sourdough in endless combinations. Even pie is made with beans! And the cookie is a mean old man when he's crossed, as when we nearly lost the chuck wagon while floating it across a river on a raft. Screaming curses too vile for a lady's ear, he was a comical sight indeed!

Fondly,
John

Hardships

July, 1872

Dear Jennie,

Already I have lost track of time, just as I was warned. Each day seems like the last—early risings, the same work and food, hardly any sleep. I do not know what day of the week this is!

Last night we buried Tom Jackson, a man of spirit and wit who was bitten by a rattlesnake. Cookie, our sourdough "doctor," did what he could, alas to no avail. We buried Tom while the stars twinkled in the cool cloudless night.

Tonight I will be one of the two "nighthawks," or night guards, and will watch the herd for two-hour shifts. I will practice the few songs I have learned while at the ranch. The restless cattle settle for the night when we hum or sing a solemn tune. We ride around the herd to make them move their bodies tightly together. They take comfort in the closeness.

We camp for the night on the open plains, with no trees nearby that can harbor wolves or rustlers. Only the lights of the campfire and lanterns pierce the darkness.

I must sleep now before it's time to perform my night duties.

Fondly,
John

Dust, Wind, and Rain

July, 1872

Dear Jennie,

Riding drag, as I do, must be the worst place to be on this earth. I and two others follow the herd. We watch for strays and fill our bellies with dust startled from the earth by the hooves of the herd. I have given up all hope of cleanliness. My clothing, boots, and bedroll are encrusted with dirt; its taste is on my tongue. My face benefits from a quick wash now and again, but I'll want to burn my clothes when we arrive in Abilene. (If they are washed, they'll fall to pieces!) Cookie gave us all a shave, which felt wonderful.

Jennie, I fear I shall die of boredom before we reach Abilene. I've begun to read the labels on Cookie's cans! Can madness lie far ahead? The days of dust are relieved only by drenching rain, or hail. The cattle become stuck in mud-filled rivers. Alas, some are drowned in the swift waters or are pulled down by quicksand. The longhorns fear the water but enjoy the mud. It offers them some relief from the insects that seek refuge in their hides—and in ours.

Twelve hours I spend in the saddle each day, but as I know how to read and write (an uncommon talent, I have found), I hope to better myself. The trail boss keeps records, and my skills would prove most useful, but I know I will need more trail experience.

Fondly,
John

JA Ranch, Texas, *Erwin E. Smith,* 1907.

47

Stampede!

August, 1872

Dear Jennie,

With Abilene only a few days away, the men are exceedingly anxious. We long for a bath, clean clothes, a warm bed—and our pay. (Henry Morton's remuneration will not last long, I'll wager, as he's oft spoken of his fondness for card games and whiskey!)

This may be my last letter for a while, sweet Jennie, at least until I've found more ranch work. But the story that now unfolds will linger long after you've read my last line. For that which all cowboys most fear—a stampede—did indeed occur.

Three nights ago, the night skies filled with lightning and the air bristled with cracking thunder. The herd became restless and was soon spooked by the storm. We all sprang from our bedrolls and into our boots. We had slept with the reins in our hands, ready for just such a need to saddle up quickly. In seconds we were racing to get to the front of the stampeding herd.

The ground trembled as the cattle hurtled into the darkness, not knowing what cliff or gorge lay ahead to consume them—and us. The heat from their bodies was stifling.

Dutch Jones reached the front of the herd after a ten-mile ride, and fired his pistol when all else failed to turn the animals. The lead cow finally turned and the herd circled on itself, spiraling until the stampede was over. We feared for our lives, Jennie, for many a cowboy has heard of men knocked from their mounts by the cattle and trampled until nothing remained to be buried.

It took lots of Texas lullabies to settle the herd for the rest of the night. The next day we found that two hundred cattle were lost that stormy night (and the rancher's money lost with them!). I am glad Abilene is so close. I will write again soon with a new address.

Fondly,
John

A cowboy's days and nights were filled with hard work, but there was time for a bit of fun on the drive, too. Some cowboys played dominoes or cards (no gambling was allowed). Some played mumblety-peg, a game where men flipped their knives into the ground and tried to get them to stand up straight. (The game was first called mumble-the-peg. Wooden pegs were used instead of knives, and the loser was expected to pull his peg out of the ground with his teeth.)

Other cowboys enjoyed riding contests. A man might try to pick up a coin from the ground while galloping by at top speed, or he might try to ride on the back of a steer. These games later became part of rodeo competitions (see page 86).

The Boss, the Cook, and the Cowboy

Remuda

Wrangler

Chuck wagon

Flank

Swing

Point

Drag

Drag

Trail boss

Drag

Flank

Swing

Point

The most important member of the cattle drive crew was the trail boss. He rode ahead of the herd, and scouted for water, pasture, and campsites along the trail. He checked the provisions, kept records, assigned duties to the men, and settled any problems, for his word was law. For all this work, the trail boss received the grand sum of about $125 a month—more than anyone else on the drive crew.

The cook was paid about $50 a month to keep the men full and happy; cowboys received about $30 and their grub.

During the drive, the herding cowboys followed the trail boss in pairs, traveling on either side of the herd. Point riders led the way, swing riders helped turn the herd, and flank riders moved alongside, watching for strays and keeping the cattle moving at a slow pace. The men often took turns at the various positions. But the drag riders, usually inexperienced cowboys, had the dustiest and most unpopular positions of all. They traveled at the back of the herd, along with the wrangler and the remuda.

Chow Time!

Hard-working cowboys needed plenty of fuel to keep going during the long weeks on the trail, and ranchers knew they had to hire the best cooks they could find to keep the men happy and productive. Many cowboys wouldn't work on a ranch where the chuck (food) wasn't tasty and plentiful.

The cook was often an older man, an ex-cowboy whose body was too broken to ride and rope any longer. He had more than enough work to keep him busy. He was the wake-up man in the morning, the handyman who could repair the chuck wagon, the "doctor" who doled out home remedies, the barber, and even the clothes-mender who sewed on buttons.

The chuck wagon was the cook's domain, and woe to anyone who crossed him. The wooden wagon was built on strong iron axles that could handle the rough trails, and it was pulled by four horses or mules.

Inside the wagon there was space to keep tools, bedding, supplies, and the chuck box. (Some ranches provided a second wagon, called a *hoodlum wagon*, to carry spare bedding, tents, saddles, and ropes.) The chuck box was built on the back of the wagon, facing out and braced by a hinged piece of wood that could be pulled down to serve as the cook's counter. This counter was for food preparation only. There were no tables out on the range, so cowboys usually ate sitting cross-legged on the ground.

The chuck box had shelves and drawers, each filled with specific items: dry goods like flour and sugar, dried fruit, beans, lard, coffee, tobacco, and some whiskey (for medicinal purposes only—and some ranchers didn't allow that item at all).

One drawer was often kept for the trail boss to use. He might have his branding book, work papers, and pencils in it. The "possible drawer" held medicine like castor oil (for constipation), liniment oil (to rub on the sore muscles of both the men and and the horses!) razors, and a sewing kit. Yet another drawer contained the "eatin' irons"—the knives, forks, spoons, tin plates, and cups.

The chuck wagon could be covered with a canvas roof. Another piece of canvas served as a rain cover that stretched over the cook as he worked at the counter. A water barrel was fastened to the side of the wagon; a box called the *boot* held the heavy skillets and pots. Under the wagon was the cooney (from the Spanish *cuna*, meaning "cradle"), a hanging sling of cowhide that held firewood or cow chips (dried dung) for cooking fuel.

Rain or shine, the cook traveled ahead of the cowboys so that the chuck would be ready when the men came off the trail. He made a campfire and hung a pot of beans over it to cook for hours. He stewed the coffee and baked the biscuits and pies in a Dutch oven (a large baking pot that sat on or beside the open fire). By the time the cowboys neared the campfire, the air was filled with the scents of the day's meal.

If you were called a dough wrangler, cookie, sourdough, bean-master, hasher, grub slinger, *or* dough-roller, *you were, without a doubt, the cook!*

Chuck, Glorious Chuck

A cowboy on the trail could count on eating plenty of beans, bread, and meat. These three items appeared on his plate in all kinds of mixtures and shapes. Early morning breakfast might be coffee and bread. Lunch and supper would be beefsteak or stew… and lots of beans.

There was always plenty of beef around, but no refrigeration. If a cow was killed on the trail, it was left to cool in the night air, and then cooked. (This was a good way to dispose of a troublesome animal that might start a dangerous stampede.)

Biscuits, dried (or, later, canned) fruits, maybe venison and molasses (called *lick*) rounded out the cowboy's diet. A pot of sourdough starter was refilled with fresh flour and water every time a scoopful was removed to make yet another loaf of bread.

Cowboys ate in shifts, always leaving someone to watch the herd. And they ate quickly, so that the next group could have its turn to eat. A man usually ate everything he took, but if he didn't, he scraped the leftovers into the fire and dropped his dirty dishes into the "wreck pan" to be washed by the cook and any available helpers. Nobody picked up after a cowboy. If a man left his dishes on the ground, they stayed there!

52

Chili

Meat stews needed plenty of cooking to break down the tough meat. And some recipes, like chili con carne (chili peppers with meat), were filled with spices to disguise the taste of old and maybe spoiled beef. Cowboys called chili *red hot* because of its peppery taste. Beans were not always added. Some cooks tossed in chicken, armadillo, and even rattlesnake meat.

A dough wrangler would have used dried beans for this dish, but you can use convenient canned kidney beans.

1 tablespoon (15 mL) vegetable oil
1 onion, chopped
1 lb (500 g) ground beef

1 tablespoon (15 mL) flour
2 19-oz (540-mL) cans red kidney beans, undrained
3 cloves garlic, crushed
2 teaspoons (10 mL) chili powder
Salt and pepper to taste

In a heavy pot over medium heat, heat the oil. Add the onion and cook for a few minutes. Add the meat and cook until well browned. Stir in the flour and cook for one minute, then add the kidney beans, garlic, chili powder, salt, and pepper. Cover and cook over low heat for about one hour. Taste and add more chili powder, salt, and pepper, if desired. Serves four.

Danger!

Cowboys on the trail had much to fear. They could be trampled during a cattle stampede, struck by lightning during a storm, bitten by rattlesnakes, or drowned while crossing a rushing river. Despite the special design of their boots (see page 36), the most common cause of death was falling off a horse and being dragged along with one foot caught in a stirrup.

Other threats included wolves, pumas, and coyotes, which could attack the herd or the horses. Bands of rustlers traveled the plains stealing cattle. Often they tricked the trail boss by claiming to be ranchers collecting their own animals. And sometimes there were attacks by the Native people, on whose territory the cowboys often trespassed.

Firearms frequently proved the only defense the cowboy

had when he was threatened by nature or by other men. Guns and rifles were used, but not as often as we might think. When a cowboy dressed up in his best clothes and posed for a photographer, he usually strapped on his holster and gun for show. But on the ranch, a cowboy seldom wore his gun. The popular 1873 Colt .45 revolver weighed more than two pounds and had a seven-and-a-half-inch barrel, so it was awkward to wear on the hip if working with the horses and cattle. Guns were needed more to deal with dangers on the trail. There, a cowboy could wear his revolver in a high-riding holster around his waist, or in a special compartment sewn into "holster chaps," so the gun didn't interfere with his riding.

A gun cost less than a saddle, but a cowboy didn't like to

shoot it any more than necessary, because ammunition was very expensive. (Some people claimed it was cheaper to hang a man than shoot him.) To save money, a man kept the empty cartridge cases after he'd fired. Later, by the campfire, he made his own bullets to fill the used cases.

Handguns were only accurate when shooting at short distances, so a carbine or rifle was carried in a special holder on the saddle for hitting targets more than seventy-five feet (twenty-five meters) away. But there were disadvantages to rifles. The popular Winchester Model 1873 added seven and a half pounds (three kilograms) to the saddle weight. A rifle was also more expensive to shoot. The lever action spit out the bullet cases, making it difficult to collect and recycle them.

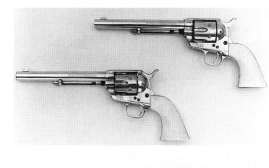

Left: *A Colt .44 "Frontier Six Shooter" revolver.* Below: *A Winchester carbine, ca. 1873.*

The End of the Trail

Abilene, Kansas, 1875.

After traveling nearly a thousand miles, cowboys were relieved to reach the cattle towns built at the railheads. Some towns were nothing but cities of tents. Others, like Abilene, Kansas, had wooden buildings, including a bank, a general store, and a hotel. But relaxation didn't begin until the dusty herds had been handed over to their new owners.

If more than one herd arrived at the railhead at the same time, the cowboys had to stay with their cattle outside town and wait for their turn with the buyers. (Men not needed to "baby-sit" the herd were allowed to go into town earlier.) During "yarding," the cattle were driven into pens and sold. Animals that had been worth three dollars a head in southern Texas could bring thirty dollars a head in the cattle town market.

After they were sold, the cattle were loaded onto railroad cars and sent to places like Chicago, where customers were waiting to buy beef. Sometimes the battered chuck wagon and cow ponies were sold, too.

Then it was time for the cowboys to be paid. They received a large sum all at once, up to one hundred dollars for their efforts. And the citizens of the cattle town were ready to help the men spend it quickly.

Boot Hill

Cattle towns throughout the Old West had a place called Boot Hill—a graveyard where outlaws and innocent people alike found their final resting place. The name came from the fact that some of the men were buried with their boots on. Others were buried with their boots placed under their heads like pillows.

In Dodge City, where the name was first used, Boot Hill was located next to the town on a high hill. Many a man was buried wrapped only in his saddle blanket, because there often wasn't enough wood on the prairies to build a coffin.

Time to Play

The saloon was usually the first building erected in a cattle town, and it was the center of social life. The main room often featured a long bar, tables and chairs, and some pictures on the wall. In Dodge City, Kansas, called Queen of the Cow Towns, the saloons and stores were open twenty-four hours a day, and their staffs worked twelve-hour shifts. Business boomed until after the year's last drive, when too few cowboys meant that some places had to close down for the winter. The homesteaders who lived in town year-round waited for the spring drives that would bring in the cowboys once again.

It was first things first when a cowboy came to town. After weeks or months on the trail, he wanted to get clean with a shave, a haircut, and a sudsy bath. Then it was off to the store for some new clothes. The trail clothes (often the same shirt

A cowboy who bellied up to the bar in a cow town might order red-eye, blue joint, tangle foot, rot gut, bug juice, breakey leg, coffin varnish, tarantula juice, or firewater—and get a serving of liquor from the bartender. The result was often what Calamity Jane called a "high lonesome," or a long drinking binge. A glass of whiskey cost "a bit," or twelve and a half cents; beer cost ten cents.

and pants for the entire trip) were ruined. A new hat and tight boots that made his feet look attractively small might be on a man's shopping list, too.

Finally, it was time to sample the cow town's entertainments. There was plenty to drink in the saloon, and lots of gambling to use any extra funds a man might have tucked away. The mixture of "tarantula juice" (whiskey) and gambling could lead to dangerous gunplay. To avoid trouble, some local laws demanded that cowboys hang up their guns when they entered the saloon. Drunken men still had brawls, but historians say that face-to-face shoot-outs were very rare, despite the scenes shown in movies. In fact, newspapers in the five major cattle towns reported only about thirty shooting deaths over a period of ten years.

Saloons, like their customers, ranged from rustic to elegant.

Prairie Nymphs

Cowboys on the trail complained of loneliness. At the end of the drive, they looked for female companionship in the saloons, where women known as prairie nymphs were anxious to meet men with lots of money in their pockets.

It was said that no respectable woman could be found in a saloon. Smoky oil lamps barely lit the main room, and the air was filled with hoots and hollers and the sounds of loud music played on the piano or fiddle. Cowboys played poker and paid women with names like Big Nose Kate, Squirrel-toothed Alice and Hambone Jane to dance with them.

In Without Knocking, *Charles M. Russell, 1909, oil on canvas.*

"DANCE-HOUSE."

Ready, Aim...Spit !

More than one spittoon, or cuspidor, was found on the floor of every saloon—and in many homes, too. These china or brass bowls had funnel tops, into which the customers spit  long streams of tobacco juice. Sometimes chewers missed the spittoon, making saloon floors dangerously slippery. Sawdust was often sprinkled on the floors to help make the cleanup a little less nasty.

Wild Bill Hickok

Belle Starr

The Law and Outlaws

When the towns of the West were first settled, many of them had no local governments and no peacekeepers. But the growth of the cattle business changed all that. The rowdiness of the cowboys in the cattle towns sometimes led to lawbreaking. Tipsy cowpunchers were caught "hurrahing" down the street, riding and shooting their pistols into the air. Riots broke out in the saloons when one man accused another of cheating at poker. Men also fought over the attentions of the local women.

Someone had to see that laws weren't broken, and that person was the law officer, with help from his assistant, the deputy. The sheriff was elected by the townspeople and was responsible for keeping the peace. He had the power to call a posse (a group of men who helped him), and he could arrest lawbreakers who were then kept in the local calaboose, or jail. The deputy helped the

James Butler Hickok
1837–1876

"Wild Bill" Hickok was a gambler, an army scout, and the creator of whopping stories about himself. He served as marshal in Kansas cowtowns, including Abilene, but lost his job because he shot both troublemakers and innocent bystanders. He was reported to be the fastest gun in the West, and after his lawman days he traveled for a short time in the East as a performer with Buffalo Bill Cody (see page 69).

Back out West, Wild Bill beat a drifter named Jack McCall at cards. A day or two later, McCall walked into the saloon where Hickok was playing poker. It was said that Hickok always sat with his back to the wall, but that day he didn't. McCall stepped up and shot him. Hickok slumped to the floor still clutching his winning hand—a queen, a pair of aces, and a pair of eights. Today, the card combination of "aces and eights" is known as a Dead Man's Hand.

Belle Starr
1848–1889

No one suspected that baby Myra Belle Shirley of Missouri would grow up to become known as the Bandit Queen. Her father was wealthy enough to send her to a private boarding school, but Belle later decided outlaws were the best companions.

Over the years, Belle lived with one desperado after another, had two children, and began to wear velvet dresses accented with a holster and pistols. She rode her horse, Venus, sidesaddle, as a "lady" should.

Belle eventually married Sam Starr, and the couple led a gang of rustlers who stole horses and cattle for resale. Many robberies were blamed on the Starrs, but after every jail sentence, they simply went back to their life of crime. After Sam's death, Belle continued to run her ranch as a hideout for outlaws. One evening, while riding alone, the Bandit Queen was ambushed and killed, perhaps by one of her own desperadoes.

Abilene, Kansas, was called "the meanest hole in the state." "The wickedest little city in America" was Dodge City.

Enter the Law,
E.C. Ward.

Calamity Jane (see page 13) claimed to have married Wild Bill, and she rode into Deadwood with him when he returned West. Twenty-seven years after Hickok's death, Jane asked to be buried next to him—and she was.

sheriff and was the acting sheriff when needed.

A marshal was an appointed official whose duties were similar to the sheriff's. He also accompanied the circuit judges, who traveled from place to place for trials.

The law officer's pay was about one hundred dollars a month. Deputies received about seventy-five dollars a month.

In fact, there was often little difference between lawmen and outlaws. They were all gunmen who used the laws (or broke them) for their own advantage. Some law officers were picked for the job because they had killed before. Some were paid a cash bonus for every arrest they made. But no matter which side of the law he was on, the successful gunslinger had to have what lawman Bat Masterson described as three qualities: the courage to fight, skill in handling his pistol, and the "cold nerve" to shoot deliberately.

OUTLAWS & LAWMEN

Bat Masterson

William Barclay Masterson
1853–1921

"Bat" Masterson was known for his stylish dress, his neat bowler hats, and his reputation as one of the most successful gamblers in the West. He won a contest for the most popular man in Dodge City in 1885. The prize was a gold-headed cane. Bat's nickname was based on the fact that he used his cane to bat, or knock, the heads of any troublemakers.

Masterson might have won a popularity contest, but he was also feared as a gunslinger and a lawman. He and his two brothers served as law officers in and around Dodge City. Bat was first Marshal Wyatt Earp's deputy and was later elected sheriff. Eventually he left Dodge City and moved to New York City, where he became a sports writer for a newspaper.

OUTLAWS & LAWMEN

Billy the Kid

Billy the Kid
(alias Henry McCarty, alias William Bonney)
1859–1881

Billy the Kid was just that—a kid. By the time he was a teenager, he had already been in trouble with the law.

Billy worked as a cowboy until his employer was killed. His desire for revenge made him a killer, too, and he soon became famous as a murderer and cattle rustler.

Pat Garrett, who was once a close friend of the Kid, was elected sheriff so that he could track Billy down. After months, he caught the outlaw, who was sentenced to be hanged. But Billy had a talent for jailbreaks, and he escaped. Still wearing his leg irons, he hobbled into the street, where he shot at guards. Then he grabbed a horse and rode away.

But even Billy the Kid couldn't run forever. Pat Garrett finally discovered him hiding out in a friend's house in New Mexico. In a darkened bedroom, Garrett shot the Kid—and became famous himself.

After the Money's Gone

After just a few days in places like Abilene, many cowpunchers were "busted." Their hard-earned cash was in the pockets of the prairie nymphs, the shopkeepers, and the bartenders. Some cowboys even had to borrow money to get out of town and back to the ranches where they worked the fall roundup, a smaller version of the spring activity.

But a number of ranches laid off many of their hired men during the winter months, and waited until spring to rehire. Most cowboys left the cow towns and drifted from place to place, picking up odd ranch jobs, or hunting wolves for bounty money. (At that time wolves were considered pests, and the government paid hunters for each animal they killed.) Some

A winter line camp in Wyoming.

men quit the cowboy life after their first drive; the romantic image of a thrilling life on the open plains had been quickly erased by the dirty and dangerous reality. Others continued to wander all over the West and north into Montana to find more work. Often these unemployed cowboys were a welcome sight on a remote ranch. In exchange for food and bed, the drifter shared the latest news and gossip, and entertained the ranch people with stories of his wild and woolly times in cow towns like Abilene.

There was still plenty to do on a ranch after the last drive of the year. Equipment was repaired or replaced. Fences were built, and the animals in the barns needed to be looked after. Or a cowboy could spend his day alone, riding the "line" (the boundaries of a large ranch) and looking for any cattle that might have strayed. Injured animals were treated; cattle caught in rocks or holes were pulled out.

In the North, about every ten miles along the boundary there was a "line camp," a crude log or sod cabin where a cowboy could warm up when he wasn't checking the herds. Grass and water supplies were constantly monitored during the fierce winter months. Ranchers needed to know how much food was available across the plains, and cowboys had to lead lost cattle through the wind and snow to exposed bits of pasture. Wearing their woolly chaps and heavy work gloves, they often had to break through ice to find water for the thirsty animals.

Winter work on a Northern ranch meant a man could spend weeks in a snowbound cabin without speaking to a soul, except the cattle. It's no wonder the cowboys got excited when winter ended and springtime promised another roundup.

Retirement

Most cowboys were young, in their late teens or early twenties. They were wiry, muscular men who could take the hard physical labor, the long hours, and the unbalanced diets on the range. The cowboy life was exciting for many, but it could quickly wear out a man and make him old before his time. Very few men worked as cowboys for longer than ten years.

Broken limbs and premature aging under the sunny skies made some cowboys retire early. Those who liked the life too much to leave it could become cooks, or help manage the ranch. Others "retired" by settling down in the towns. There they married, raised families, and worked in small businesses.

Some cowboys used their savings and years of experience to start ranching for themselves. And still others became homesteaders, claiming land and operating farms.

Dodge City, 1879.

Part III

THE CLOSING OF THE WEST

The End of the Cattle Boom

By 1886 millions of cattle had been delivered to the Northern railheads—and Eastern dinner tables. Ranchers had become rich, and cowboys had never been busier. But the heyday of these cowpunchers was over. By the early 1880s, the price of beef began to fall. There were more cattle than people wanted to buy. The ranchers had been too successful. Herds that had once sold for more than thirty dollars a head were suddenly worth only seven dollars each.

But the falling demand for beef was not the only reason for the end of the cattle boom. Kansas closed its borders to Southern cattle because longhorns carried "Texas fever," a disease that could be passed on to dairy cattle. And three other items led to the downfall of the cowboy: wire, sheep, and snow.

Wire

After the Homestead Act of 1862 was passed, settlers flocked to the West to farm the vast land. Anyone who farmed 160 acres (65 hectares) of unclaimed land and lived on it for five years could call the property his own. This meant the ranchers had no legal right to the open prairie where their herds usually grazed until the roundup.

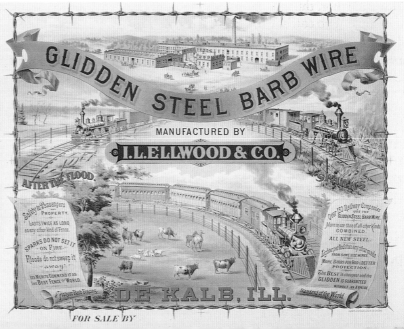

The open range areas began to shrink as homesteaders (also called "sodbusters" or "nesters") fenced in their new claims. It was difficult to find enough wood on the prairies to build the miles of fences needed to contain the farm properties, but in 1874 an Illinois farmer, Joseph Glidden (1813–1906), patented barbed wire and changed the face of the West.

Barbed wire was perfect for fencing in large areas. It was strong, tough, and cheap. The sharp twists of wire reminded cattle, horses, or men that they had gone too far.

The fencing done by ranchers caused problems, because the lands sometimes weren't legally theirs. Some ranchers tried to outwit the government and claimed to be homesteaders in order to keep their land. Violence often broke out between the sodbusters and the ranchers.

The new fences meant that cowboys weren't needed for huge roundups anymore, since the fenced-in herds couldn't stray very far. And the railroads now ran closer to the cattle-raising areas. Soon only a few men were needed to drive herds from the fenced pastures to the railcars just a short distance away.

It was time for the cowboy to move on.

Sheep

Homesteaders weren't the only rivals the cattle ranchers had on the prairies. Sheepherders also wanted their flocks to have a share of the grazing land.

Ranchers claimed that the sheep cropped the grass too close to the ground, leaving little for the cattle to eat. This meant thinner cattle, and thin cattle sold for less. Since the ranchers had been on the land first and believed they were therefore the owners, they harassed the sheepherders and told them to leave the land. If the sheepherders refused, violent action was often the result. Vicious battles between the sheep ranchers and cattle ranchers continued for years. Sheep were poisoned, and entire flocks were destroyed.

But the "sheep wars" were fought for control of a range that was quickly disappearing in any case. The battles between the sheep herders and cattle ranchers lasted until the early 1900s. Eventually, ranchers saw that sheep could be good for pastureland, too. Their hooves turned the soil, and their droppings richly fed the grasses the cattle enjoyed.

Snow

In the Northern states, cattle wandered over the range during the winter months, monitored by the bundled-up cowboys. They nibbled at the grasses that remained, and they drank from the half-frozen water holes and streams. During the winter of 1886–87, however, the snows in Montana came early and fell so deep that the cattle could find no food. Blizzards lasted for days, and the cowboys couldn't get outside to take hay to the herds. Temperatures dipped far below freezing. Cattle froze, or were buried alive. After the spring thaw, Northern ranchers learned that more than half of their cattle had starved or frozen to death.

For ranchers who were already faced with the loss of grazing land and low beef prices, the "big die-up" was the final straw. Many closed down, leaving fewer jobs.

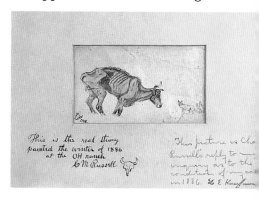

Waiting for a Chinook, *Charles M. Russell, 1886, watercolor on paper.*

Part IV

BUILDING THE COWBOY MYTH

The Virginian

Owen Wister's 1902 novel, *The Virginian*, was a good example of Wild West mania. Wister (1860–1935) was a lawyer from Philadelphia, Pennsylvania. He suffered from poor health, and on his doctor's advice he traveled to Wyoming, where the dry, sunny climate was supposed to be more healthful. There he filled journals with notes about cowboy life, and eventually he wrote *The Virginian*.

Readers didn't care that the Virginian wasn't a true historical cowboy. There was heroism, love interest, and a villain to keep them turning the pages. The book quickly became one of the most widely read novels in America. Fifty thousand copies were sold in just two months.

Dustin Farnum as the Virginian in the 1904 stage version of the novel.

Although the days of open-range ranching had ended by 1890, the world's interest in cowboys was growing. But the hard-working, true-life cowboy was often forgotten. Instead, tourists and reporters took home thrilling tales of adventure and wild lawbreaking. These exciting but exaggerated stories were eagerly accepted as truth, and the rest of the world begged for more.

Some of the earliest creators of this romantic view of the cowboy were the writers of dime novels that flooded the market. These inexpensive books were filled with tales of derring-do—most of it invented. Sometimes real-life figures like Wild Bill Hickok or Buffalo Bill were the main characters, but the plots were not true. For example, Native people were often cast as the villains in western novels, and this attitude was carried into later plays and films. It is accepted by some people even today, causing a great deal of pain for the Native community.

Sometimes real cowboys like Teddy Blue Abbott and Charles Siringo wrote in detail about their lives. These autobiographies remained popular for many years, but in general the historical cowboy began to disappear. Instead, the invented cowboy jumped from the pages of books and magazines. And still the public wanted more.

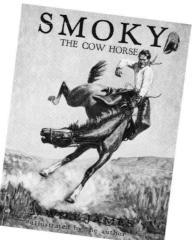

A True Cowboy Myth

"I was born in Montana. When I let out my first squawk there was only a few inches of quilting between me and the prairie sod, my first squint at sunlight was under a canvas flap and the first sounds that came to my ears was the jingling of my dad's spurs, the nickering of horses, and the bellering of cattle."

That's how author Will Roderick James described his birth in 1892. *Lone Cowboy*, his life story, is filled with dramatic incidents: his birth on the open prairie, the death of both his parents by the time he was four, his adoption by a French-Canadian trapper, his time spent on ranches, and his work as a stunt man in western movies.

In 1927 James won the Newbery Medal for his popular novel *Smoky*, the story of a cowboy and his horse. Films were made of the book, and many boys were named after the story's main character, Clint. Other books followed, although some say *Smoky* remained his best.

Will James died in Hollywood in 1942. In 1967, however, people learned that he had made up more than his novels. His real name was in fact Joseph Ernest Nephtali Dufault, and he was born of French-speaking parents in Quebec, Canada. As a boy, he read all he could about the West, and then he set out to live the cowboy life. He changed his name more than once before settling on Will James, although his drifting cowboy career and movie stunt work were true.

In spite of his invented past, James's books continue to give western fans a wonderful glimpse of the "proper cowboy."

Come One, Come All

William F. Cody (1846–1917) spread the romantic image of the cowboy around the world. Frontiersman Cody earned the nickname "Buffalo Bill" after he became known for single-handedly shooting more than four thousand buffalo in order to supply meat to railroad workers in the West.

When the public began showing an interest in cowboys and horses, Cody saw a golden opportunity. In 1883 he organized a show called Buffalo Bill's Wild West and Congress of Rough Riders of the World, and the next year Cody's troupe, which included the famous Sioux leader, Sitting Bull, began traveling around North America.

During the three-hour show, actor-cowboys dressed in their costume finery (not *real* cowboy clothes) and acted out frontier events like stagecoach robberies and cavalry battles. There was roping and riding, fancy shooting demonstrations, and plenty of young women for the valiant cowboys to "rescue" from evil villains. Mexican vaqueros demonstrated how to throw bolas (a form of lasso), and shouted loudly in Spanish. This was all new and exciting for spectators, who didn't care how authentic the entertainment was. To them, this was the real West.

Europeans soon joined in the hoopla. In 1887 Buffalo Bill was invited to entertain England's Queen Victoria. Two hundred actors and hundreds of animals sailed to London to help the queen celebrate fifty years on the throne.

Eventually other businessmen launched their own shows, which remained popular until World War I and the coming of the movies drew people's attention elsewhere. In 1916, Buffalo Bill's production closed down. Cody died a year later, deeply in debt.

Sitting Bull and Buffalo Bill Cody.

69

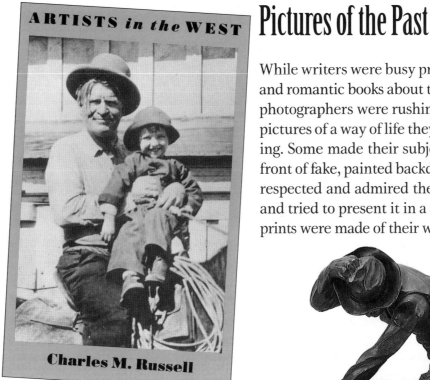

ARTISTS in the WEST

Frederic Remington

ARTISTS in the WEST

Charles M. Russell

Pictures of the Past

While writers were busy producing unbelievable and romantic books about the cowboy, artists and photographers were rushing to the West to make pictures of a way of life they knew was disappearing. Some made their subjects pose in studios in front of fake, painted backdrops. But other artists respected and admired the cowboy's way of life, and tried to present it in a true way. Inexpensive prints were made of their works, which were soon found in many North American homes.

Frederic Remington
1861–1909

Artist Frederic Remington was born in New York State and educated at Yale Art School, but like his friend Owen Wister, he went west for his health and fell in love with the area. He worked as a cowboy and sheep rancher, and by the time he was thirty, his sketches of Western life had made him famous. Remington was called an artist-historian because of his attention to the details of a cowboy's clothing and horses. He produced nearly three thousand drawings and paintings and twenty-five bronze sculptures that captured the historical cowboy forever.

Charles M. Russell
1864–1926

Self-taught painter Charles Russell was called *the* cowboy artist. Born in Missouri, Russell went west to become a cowboy when he was fifteen. He once said, "For eleven years I sung to the horses and cattle." Like Remington, he recorded scenes of cowboy and Native life around him. His work was filled with fine details and a sense of humor. He was particularly fond of depicting the buffalo hunt, and by 1911 his paintings and sculptures of the Old West were selling in New York City.

Erwin E. Smith

Photographer Erwin E. Smith (1886–1947) was born in Texas just as the huge cattle drives ended. But Smith admired cowboys and learned all he could about them. He spent twenty-five years in ranch life, taking thousands of photographs of cowboys by sun, moon, and campfire light. His black-and-white photos show the dusty herds and hard-working men who carried on even after the era of the cowboy had ended.

IS Ranch, Texas, *Erwin E. Smith, 1908. The photographer took this self-portrait when he stopped at the chuck wagon for a cup of coffee.*

Left: The Rattlesnake, *Frederic Remington, 1905, cast bronze.*
Right: Sun River War Party, *Charles M. Russell, 1903, oil on canvas.*

The Changing Western

Audiences were stunned during the silent film The Great Train Robbery *(1903) when the actor fired his gun straight at the camera in the final scene.*

Almost everyone has seen at least one western movie. For many people, the western has formed a lot of their ideas about life in cowboy days.

But the cowboy movie has changed a great deal over the years. The West we see in the 1992 film *Unforgiven*, would have seemed very unfamiliar to our grandparents.

Westerns were among the first movies ever made. And the West, as it was shown in those early films, was a place of heroes (good guys who often wore white hats) and bad guys (who were either bandits or Natives or Mexicans—or all three). Cowboys were rarely dirty; as time went on, actors like Tom Mix began to dress up in incredibly fancy clothes that would have seemed bizarre to a real cowboy.

The romantic image of the cowboy was not the only unrealistic portrait created by western mythmakers. From the beginning of such western entertainments as the dime novel and Wild West shows, Native people of North America were treated unfairly, and this carried over into the way Natives were portrayed in films. The attitude also spilled into backyards around the world, where children eagerly played "cowboys and Indians" and were happy when the villainous "redskins" were defeated by the men in white hats.

In recent years, the aboriginal people of North America have been working to educate the rest of the world about their history. But there are many years of untruths to correct.

Native parts in early films were often played by white actors dressed in ridiculous costumes and makeup that made the "Indian" either a laughingstock or the worst villain in the universe. "Indians" were barbaric savages who grunted "ugh" and "how," and scared women and children with blood-curdling screams. The creativity and intelligence of the people were ignored. Instead, they were shown trading beads and blankets, frightened by newfangled inventions.

Through the years, things changed somewhat. Filmmakers sometimes hired Natives to play "Indian" roles, but the characters were still demeaned by the attitudes of the times. In the

Today, performers like Tantoo Cardinal (Divided Loyalties) *are helping to change the way Natives are shown in movies.*

1960s, the "Indian" became a noble character in movies, but once again Native actors were put aside for popular box-office stars. Even Elvis Presley was cast as a half-breed.

In the 1960s and 1970s, people began to question the way Natives were portrayed. Perhaps the marauders had been the settlers and ranchers, not the Native people. Perhaps the promises made to the Natives had been false, and the Native attacks had been provoked and justified.

In recent years, filmmakers have attempted to show Native people in a more truthful and dignified way. More attention has been given to their rich traditions. Native actors have been hired to play Native and non-Native dramatic roles. Still, some argue that the situation won't be fully corrected until Native people themselves are able to tell their own stories by making their own movies.

People also started to wonder whether the settling of the West was really as simple as they had believed. They questioned the fake glamour of cowboy life and the fistfights, killing, and shooting that were such a popular part of the early westerns.

Movies began to show the West in a more complicated way. The "good guys" didn't always win, and realistic clothing, sets, and characters became much more important. The western became a way for filmmakers to make statements about the way they saw the world. Because of this, none of us will ever see the West in quite the same way again.

While Native people have been portrayed as villains in the world of entertainment, other groups have also been demeaned and underestimated. Although many cowboys were African American, they seldom appear in western films. In early western movies, Mexican characters were often introduced as sidekicks of the hero. They were dressed in outlandish costumes, wearing oversize hats and stumbling over their serapes (blanket-cloaks). While the lead actor rode a tall, spotless stallion, his Mexican companion sat upon (or fell off) a clumsy, balking donkey.

The same nation that gave the world the talented vaquero is mocked each time western stories and films portray Mexicans as fools. Likewise, many movies would have us believe that the women of the West were equally unworthy. Women were shown as disloyal girlfriends, immodest saloon girls, or tough crones who could run a ranch "like a man."

The truth is that women helped to settle the West, and they faced great hardships and danger while struggling to survive. The contributions of the African Americans, the Mexicans, and the women of the time have yet to be fully and honestly explored in the movies.

On the Screen

William S. Hart (1870-1946) was a stage and film actor. He knew and respected the West, and, unlike most of the cowboy actors of his time, he was known for showing audiences the rough, tough aspects of cowboy life. There was plenty of dust in his films and no fancy duds; he liked to wear real cowboy clothes. Hart made cowboy films from 1914 until 1925.

10209-8

COURTESY OF PARAMOUNT PICTURES

Burt Lancaster and Kirk Douglas in Gunfight at the OK Corral *(1957).*

Tom Mix (1880-1940) took William Hart's place as the top western movie star. Mix had been a soldier, a rodeo rider, and a law officer. But, unlike Hart, he didn't try to be realistic in his westerns. He wanted to show audiences a hero who could take care of villains quickly.

74

Alan Ladd and Brandon de Wilde
in Shane *(1953).*

Marlon Brando in
One-Eyed Jacks *(1961).*

Clint Eastwood in
Unforgiven *(1992).*

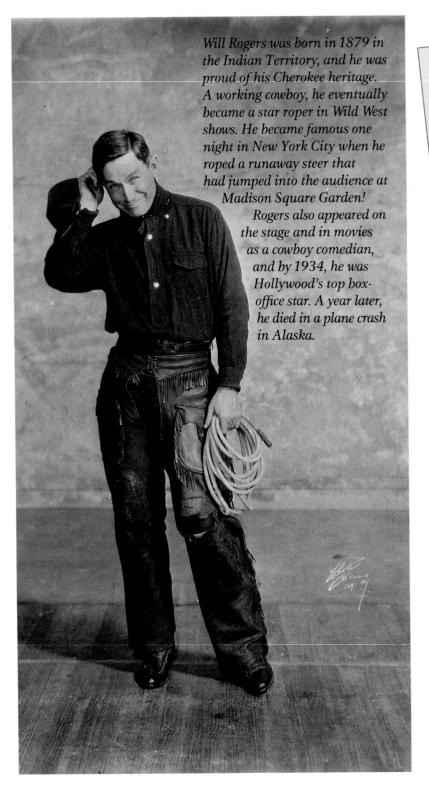

Will Rogers was born in 1879 in the Indian Territory, and he was proud of his Cherokee heritage. A working cowboy, he eventually became a star roper in Wild West shows. He became famous one night in New York City when he roped a runaway steer that had jumped into the audience at Madison Square Garden!

Rogers also appeared on the stage and in movies as a cowboy comedian, and by 1934, he was Hollywood's top box-office star. A year later, he died in a plane crash in Alaska.

Gene Autry's Cowboy Commandments

During World War II (1939–1945) many North American men were away at war. For their children, cowboy actors in afternoon movies almost became on-screen dads who offered advice, comfort, and a good example. Singing western star Gene Autry provided these ten rules for young fans who wanted to be good cowboys as well as patriotic defenders of their country:

1. [A cowboy] must not take unfair advantage of an enemy.
2. He must never go back on his word.
3. He must always tell the truth.
4. He must be gentle with children, elderly people, and animals.
5. He must not possess racially or religiously intolerant ideas.
6. He must help people in distress.
7. He must be a good worker.
8. He must respect women, parents, and his nation's laws.
9. He must neither drink nor smoke.
10. He must be a patriot.

Billy the Kid had obviously never heard of these cowboy commandments back in the 1870s!

KF 43   *Gene Autry*   Rep. Pict.

''Happy trails to you...''

The fancy clothes worn by some screen cowboys seemed positively plain when Roy Rogers rode Trigger onto the set of his show. Sequins, metal studs, and swinging fringes decorated his outfits. Rogers, a singer, and his wife, Dale Evans, were popular in western films and later on television. Trigger was known as "the smartest horse in the movies," and he performed counting tricks on the program, tapping the ground with his hoof. Children could buy Roy and Dale paper dolls, songbooks, scarves, flashlights, and watches. For nearly twenty years, Roy Rogers was King of the Cowboys for television viewers.

Cowboy Movies on Video

These good western films are available on video cassette:

High Noon *(1952)*
One of the greatest westerns of all, featuring classic conflicts between good and bad, courage and cowardice.

Shane *(1953)*
A boy's family is befriended and saved by a gunfighter who ultimately cannot change his ways.

Gunfight at the OK Corral *(1957)*
The unlikely friendship between good guy Wyatt Earp and the disreputable Doc Holliday brings this tragedy to life.

The Magnificent Seven *(1960)*
Another western classic in which a varied cast of characters comes to the rescue of a small town under attack by bandits.

Cat Ballou *(1965)*
One of the few westerns in which a woman bandit is at the center of the action. It's fun, too.

Butch Cassidy and the Sundance Kid *(1969)*
A rollicking treatment of mythic western gangsters which is both funny and sad.

77

Building a Western

The people who make modern western movies spend a great deal of time and money trying to convince audiences that what they are seeing is real. The production designer is the person who is responsible for the way a movie looks.

The production designer's job begins long before the actors come on the scene. A designer might take a month to research the Old West period, flying to different locations to see what old towns look like and studying old photographs in the movie studio's library.

Western movies can be made in different places. Outdoor scenes can be shot in the countryside; town scenes may be filmed in a real town with old-style buildings, while the modern parts of the town are removed or covered up. Sometimes the film is made on a studio set (in the early westerns, even the outdoor scenes were shot inside buildings). But often a set is specially built for just one film.

First the designer draws a design for the town. Then the set is constructed. By using different camera angles and close-ups, and by filming the action from many directions, the filmmakers can make a four-block set seem four times as large.

Everything the viewer will see is made to look real, right down to the last doorknob. Planks are aged with stains, and hit with chains or scraped to look like worn boards. Lamps, horse hitches, water troughs, and store signs are all carefully reproduced. Windows are made to look dirty and cracked, but they aren't always made of real glass, especially when the script calls for a fierce fistfight in which chairs and bodies will go flying. Instead, fake glass is used.

Fake glass was once made from sugar. Today, when actors are hit over the head with bottles or are pushed through windows, the glass is actually a kind of resin, or chemical substance, that breaks like real glass but isn't sharp enough to cut.

Other parts of the set may be doctored for a fight scene. Furniture and banister railings may sometimes be made of lightweight balsa wood, with parts of them cut almost all the way through so they will break easily. Clever photography and paints disguise the cuts and fool the viewers.

Even though a movie set may look as real as an actual Old West town, many of the buildings are probably "false fronts." When an actor opens a door to walk into a building, there may be nothing but open field on the other side. In the finished movie, audiences will see him enter a completely different, indoor set, located in a soundstage back at the studio.

But some parts of the set will be made up of "practical sets." These buildings have both an exterior *and* an interior, allowing the camera to film shots showing the outside and inside of a building, through doors and windows.

Building a movie set can cost millions of dollars. It can take as many as two hundred people three months to build a western town about four blocks long. And what happens when the filming is over? Sometimes the set is simply destroyed, because designers of other western films will want to create their own visions of the Old West. Or they may want to use the backlots of film studios, a much cheaper and more convenient option. For example, there is a five-acre western area on the property of Paramount studios. The Disney studio also has a western street and a ranch set. These sets are left up, and can be redressed for each movie.

Today, to save money and reduce waste, buildings from some movie sets are recycled. Sometimes they are donated as

Filming a saloon scene at night.

Below: *Filming* Cheyenne Autumn *(1964).*

housing or community centers, and are moved whole to new locations.

Although production designers today usually try to make their sets look as real as possible, over the years filmmakers have often fiddled with history. Movie good guys always wore white hats, and the bad guys often wore black. Many movie cowboys made their dramatic entrances into saloons through swinging gate-type doors, when real Old West saloons had ordinary glass-and-wood doors. And tense shoot-outs between the film hero and villain regularly cleared citizens from the streets, even though historians tell us that such showdowns were in fact quite rare.

Still, audiences loved to watch shoot-outs, so moviemakers tried hard to make these scenes look as believable as possible. By the 1960s, the squib was developed to make bullet wounds look real. This small explosive charge is detonated either by small batteries that are strapped to the actor or by wires from a control board or radio.

But where's all the blood?

Latex "blood bags" are filled with a red gelatin fluid and are attached to the squibs. When the gunshot is fired and the actor is "hit," the squib is detonated, and the bag bursts open. That's when the wounded cowboy drops, clutching his stained chest.

Ride 'em, Cowboy

As more and more people bought television sets in the 1950s and 1960s, cowboys became so popular that dress-up boxes almost always contained cowboy costumes and fixings. Most family albums from those days include photos of a few young buckaroos.

Alison

Stuart

Dan

Linda

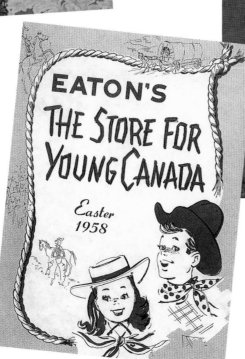

Kelly

More than Texas Lullabies

Cowboys and music have been a winning combination for more than one hundred years. During the long drives, cowboys sang Texas lullabies—mournful tunes without words—to calm the cattle at night. During the day, they sang faster pieces to quicken the pace of the herd. Some ranchers reportedly even hired minstrel groups who traveled with the herds and played to quiet them.

Cowpunchers who could play the harmonica, the fiddle, or the guitar were welcome on the trail or at the ranch, especially during long winter nights in the bunkhouse. Around the campfire, the group would sing old tunes (some dated back to England in the 1600s) and add new verses—many in poor taste.

Today, traditional cowboy songs are being rediscovered by recording artists around the world. Rock stars like Canada's Mitsou sing of "Mon Cowboy," and make videos filled with cowboy props and costumes. Even *Sesame Street* has cowboy characters who introduce western songs to preschoolers.

The Dodge City Cowboy Band.

Yo-de-lay-eee-ooo

Singing cowboys like Wilf Carter (also called Montana Slim) included yodeling in their songs. When a singer yodels, the voice moves quickly between a normal and a very high pitch. Nonsense words are often used too.

Which Red River?

From this valley they say you are going,
I will miss your bright eyes and sweet smile.
For they say you are taking the sunshine
That has brightened our pathway awhile.
Come and sit by my side if you love me.
Do not hasten to bid me adieu.
But remember the Red River Valley
And the cowboy that loves you so true.

It was once thought that the river in this traditional cowboy love song was the Red River in Texas-Oklahoma cattle territory. But research has revealed that the song refers to the Red River in Manitoba, Canada—the scene of the Rebellion of 1869, when the Métis fought to set up an independent government.

The song was sung by traders in Manitoba and spread into the northern plains. By the 1880s, it was heard on the cattle ranges, but the words, like those of many old favorites, sometimes changed as the song traveled across the countryside.

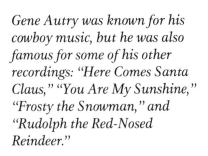

Gene Autry was known for his cowboy music, but he was also famous for some of his other recordings: "Here Comes Santa Claus," "You Are My Sunshine," "Frosty the Snowman," and "Rudolph the Red-Nosed Reindeer."

Celebrating the Cowboy Around the World

The cowboy is still a popular figure all over the world. In France, children read about the adventures of Lucky Luke, l'homme qui tire plus vite que son ombre ("the man who shoots faster than his shadow").

When carnival time comes in France, cowboy costumes are still a favorite.

Daniel

People all over the world continue to be fascinated by the cowboy. In bars that have been decorated to look like western saloons, customers can ride mechanical bulls—adult versions of the coin-operated horse rides children find in malls and supermarkets. Every year, thousands of tourists watch a modern version of Buffalo Bill's Wild West at Euro Disney in France. The Japanese are planning to build an Old West entertainment park near Tokyo. North American adventure camps sell washable-paint bullets for showdowns between players who dress up in western-style outfits.

Each spring, thousands of men, women, and children in Germany spend a week "reliving" the times of "der wilde Westen." They live in tepees or lean-tos, start fires without matches, and sometimes speak with a Texas drawl. Many even make their own costumes, trying to copy every historical detail, right down to the last porcupine quill and brass button.

Elsewhere, thousands of authentic cowboy-poets celebrate the cowpuncher's life at gatherings held every year in Elko, Nevada, and Pincher Creek, Alberta. Sometimes European television companies film the proceedings and show them to western fans abroad. Cowboy poetry began when riders sat around the campfire and passed the time by making up and reciting "rawhide sonnets." Their poems told stories of roping gigantic steers, deadly tumbles from a horse, and bone-chilling rides through wintry blizzards. Today, men and women continue to gather together to recite by heart old and new pieces that celebrate the real life of the cowboy.

Does *everyone* want to be a cowboy? The advertisers would have us believe so. Ever since the late 1800s, manufacturers have used the Old West to sell their products. Cars have been named after mustangs, pintos, colts, rangers, frontier wagons, and broncos. Perfumes and after-shaves, jewelry, toys, video games, and even bathtubs have used the cowboy's tough image to attract customers. Hats, pants, and firearms are still made by the companies that supplied the cowboy more than a century ago— J.B. Stetson, Levi Strauss, and Colt.

Restaurants serve Tex-Mex meals; fabric, bedding, and clothes feature cactus and coyote designs. Furniture is made from wagon wheels and canvas. Schools give lessons in western line-dancing, and video companies offer taped lessons for those who can't get to the schools.

The Cowboy's Circus

The word rodeo *is pronounced* RO-dee-oh *in the American Northwest and* ro-DAY-oh *in the Southwest. In western Canada, the competition is also called a stampede.*

It's hard to say when rodeos began. Cowboys working on the ranches would compete against one another at roundups and during their free time. Who could rope a calf the fastest? Who could stay on a bucking bronc the longest? Who could perform fancy tricks while riding a horse at full speed?

Once the ranges were fenced, the Wild West shows (and there were many of them) gave the out-of-work cowboy a place to "show his stuff"—and pick up some pay. Soon rodeos, or cowboy contests, became part of Western county fairs. Contestants traveled from one competition to another. Some cowboys became rodeo stars, and, later, movie stars.

Today, rodeo cowboys are professional athletes who compete for a living. They pay fees to ride in the rodeos, and if they don't do well enough to win a prize, they don't make any money. Throughout the rodeo season, they travel up to 150,000 miles (240,000 kilometers) a year. It has been calculated that a cowboy has to compete in at least one hundred rodeos a year to have even a chance at winning a world title.

For some, the rodeo life means constant fast-food meals and motel beds. In many ways, the loneliness of the old riding trail is still a part of these cowboys' lives. After only seconds out in the arena, it's time to move on to another city, another rodeo.

But the challenge of competing against an animal and the clock is enough to keep the men in the saddle—and to keep the myth of the Old West cowboy alive.

Bareback Bronc Riding

Rodeos often start with this event, which uses horses smaller than saddle bronc mounts. (The wildest broncs, fastest calves, and strongest steers are especially chosen for rodeos.)

Even before the gate to the arena is opened, the rider has to use great skill and strength to control the horse; otherwise, he is in danger of being crushed against the sides of the chute (holding pen). In the arena, the rider must spur the horse often and stay astride, with legs flying, until a horn signals the end of the ride. Bareback bronc riding is the most physically demanding rodeo event and the most dangerous, because the rider has no saddle.

Saddle Bronc Riding

In this event the bronc rider has a saddle, but riders are not allowed to use their own saddles. If they did, they might have an unfair advantage because of their saddlemakers' skills. Instead, saddles are provided, and they are all the same model.

When the gate opens, the rider holds on with only one hand as the animal tries to buck him off.

Calf Roping

In this event, the horse is more important than the man. The animal has to be very quick. The rider (on horseback) and the calf are released from the chutes, and the race is on. The rider uses a lariat and a pigging string—a shorter rope used to tie the calf's feet. The rider holds the pigging string in his teeth until the calf is caught.

Once the rider ropes the calf, he gets off his horse, throws the calf to the ground, and ties three of its feet together. The tie must hold for six seconds.

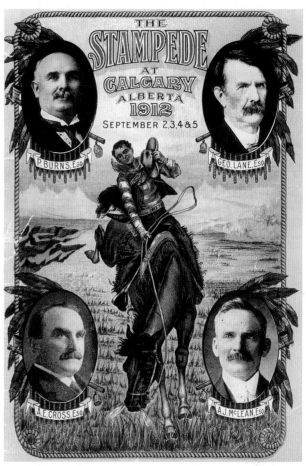

The Calgary Stampede

Each summer, one million people travel from around the world to Alberta, Canada, for the Calgary Stampede. In 1912, a young rider named Guy Weadick, along with other organizers, put together a "monster celebration"—a "tribute to all those grand old men [cowboys] whom we all delight to honor." The result was the first Stampede. Ropers and riders were given sets of rules to follow, and prize money if they won their events (silver belt buckles have also been traditional rodeo prizes).

Today, Stampede visitors can watch cowboys compete in traditional roping and riding events over ten days, and enjoy a two-hour parade, fireworks, world championship chuck-wagon racing, and grandstand musical productions. In Calgary, the early cowboys' simple contests have become the Greatest Outdoor Show on Earth.

Young Riders

Because ranch children as young as six know how to rope and tie a calf, it seems natural to have rodeo contests for them to compete in. Contenders can learn from the experts on ranches, or at a rodeo school. The young athletes have to train hard. They must develop concentration, be physically fit, and learn how to deal with strange animals. Special plastic mouthguards can be worn for safety, and heavy leather chaps give legs extra protection.

In 1961, the National Little Britches Rodeo Association was formed to help young rodeo enthusiasts. Today, junior rodeos involving almost twenty thousand contestants between eight and seventeen years old are held around North America. A youngster can move from the Little Britches events into collegiate rodeos, and then into the professional rodeo arena.

A junior rodeo cowboy of thirteen might enter the bull-riding contest. The cowboy will sit on a half-ton bull inside a pen, waiting for the animal to burst out into the arena and then try to buck the rider off its back. The junior cowboy must hold onto a rope with one hand, and stay on the bull for six awesome seconds while the animal bucks, kicks, and spins. Then the rider waits to hear the judges' results, hoping to win some of the money, saddles, belt buckles, and boots that are the prizes.

Teenagers compete in a junior rodeo in Alberta. Above: *Andy Many Fingers wrestles a steer.* Below left: *Kym Foley does a flying dismount in the goat-tying competition.* Below right: *Casey Ingram in the bareback event.*

Rodeo organizers try to protect the horses and cattle during competitions, and the animals are usually in the arena for only a short time. The Rodeo Cowboy Association has rules to protect the animals. For instance, calves must have reached a certain weight before they are used in roping events. Some people claim that rodeos hurt animals, no matter what conditions are met. To many cowboys, though, the hurt is just part of the show, as it was in the days of roping and branding on the range.

Cowgirls

There have been women bronc riders, bull riders, steer wrestlers, and trick ropers and riders since the early 1900s. Today, girls as young as eight compete in rodeos. The women's events are often separated from the men's competitions because women usually need lighter animals than men.

Many girls compete in the barrel-riding contests. It takes a well-trained horse and a skilled rider to travel in a cloverleaf pattern around the barrels at top speed. Others ride a course slalom-style in the pole-bending races. There's also a trail course, where riders complete a series of tasks, like opening a gate while on horseback. Or there's the goat-tying competition, where the contestant has to ride up to a goat, dismount, and tie together three of its legs.

Florence LaDue.
Champion Lady Fancy Roper of the World.
Stampede Calgary 1912.

Clowning Around

During a rodeo, spectators will often see clowns performing at the edge of the arena. The clowns keep the audience entertained, but they also have a serious job. If a rider falls off his horse or steer, the rodeo clowns jump into action. Dressed in bright costumes, the clowns distract the animal until the rider is safely out of the way. This can be dangerous, but the clowns are professionals and know how to dance safely around an animal's sharp horns.

The clowns' costumes are baggy so that they can move quickly, and they wear cleated running shoes instead of big circus-clown shoes that could trip them.

Most rodeo clowns were once cowboys themselves, and some still compete in the rodeo circuit. Traditionally, only men were cowboy clowns. But in 1980, Robin Sindorf became America's first female rodeo clown.

African American cowboy Bill Pickett (1860–1932) is credited with inventing steer-wrestling, originally called *bulldogging*. Bulldoggers were usually taller and heavier cowboys, because they had to have great strength to bring the bull to the ground.

Bill Pickett supposedly leapt from his horse onto the horns of a running steer and stopped it in its tracks. Then he bit the lip of the animal to distract it, and twisted it to the ground. Some reports claim that Pickett didn't even have to touch the animal with his hands

That Bulldoggin' Bill Pickett

once he had made lip contact.

There's no lip-biting these days, but bulldoggers still have to wrestle a fast, sharp-horned steer to the ground as quickly as possible in the rodeo arena. All four feet must be sticking out in the same direction, and the animal must be flat on its side.

Bill Pickett traveled with a Wild West show in the 1890s and had a long career as a bulldogger. He died in 1932, after being kicked by a horse.

Part V

COWBOYS TODAY

The New Generation

Jessica Chalmers is thirteen years old, and she has lived on ranches all her life. She represents the fourth generation of her family to live on the Chalmers Ranch in Millarville, Alberta. The ranch once covered three thousand acres in the foothills near Calgary, but has been divided and is now smaller. Jessica's grandparents, who still live on the original ranch, now have about two hundred head of cattle, which her cowboy father, Doug, helps herd.

It's spring, and Jessica shares her story of life on a ranch:

"I've been riding horses since I could barely sit up on one. By the time I was three, I was riding around my grandfather's ranch. Now I like to ride my grandfather's horse, Jack. He's a big quarter horse, chestnut-colored and seventeen hands high. I've been lucky. I've never gotten sore from riding, even after chasing cattle or riding a long time. The best thing about living on a ranch is that you can go riding whenever you want!

"All of my friends live on ranches, but we go to school in Calgary. I'm in grade seven. I want to be a veterinarian when I'm older. You can't just ranch now. You have to go to university, get a degree, *and* ranch. Veterinarians can travel and work on many ranches. They can help the cows when they have problems with their calves.

"The cattle on the ranch are purebred Salers. It's calving time now. There'll be about a hundred calves. Sometimes I have a favorite. Like Gracie. Her mother stepped on her after she was born, and I took care of her.

"I do some roping with my friends. We practice by catching the dummy [a log with a head] with our lariats. It's good practice for the team roping we do. In team roping, two riders, one on each side of a running calf, try to rope the animal. The 'header' tries to rope the neck, and the 'heeler' ropes two ankles. I'm a good header but not a good heeler. The heeler has to be very quick to rope the moving feet. We're timed, and have to be as fast as possible. If we only catch one ankle, extra seconds are added to our score, and we can lose.

"My friends and I rope in contests held at my grandfather's outdoor arena in Millarville every Wednesday during the summer. Lots of kids compete for prizes. My mother and I won a roping trophy before I was born. While she was expecting me, she roped a steer in a rodeo!

"When I was about nine years old, I helped out on my first roundup. We woke up about four o'clock in the morning and worked until noon. Then we ate lunch on the side of the road; my grandmother makes the best chili in the world! Then back to work all afternoon. Because the roundup was near the ranch, I could go home at night and sleep in my soft bed instead of on the ground.

"When people ask what's the worst part about living on a ranch, I say there's *no* worst part. My friends and I go riding together a lot, and have even visited dude ranches with some of our friends who live in Calgary. It's funny to watch the city riders at the dude ranches. They just want to run, run, run. They race around on their horses, and don't like to just trot.

"City kids are sometimes surprised when they visit our ranch. Ranch kids sometimes wear cowboy hats, but not all the time. And I only wear cowboy boots for protection when I'm going to ride. I don't wear spurs when I ride, because if you have a good horse you don't need them. When I'm not riding, I like to play the saxophone and watch the latest *Star Trek* television shows—not the old ones! And I'd like to be a pilot like my mother. Maybe I'll be a flying veterinarian!"

The New Old West

A cowboy poet once remarked, "In some ways, we're born a hundred years too late. In other ways, we're a reminder of something in danger of being lost." The cowboy of the Old West is certainly a part of the world's legends, but he is not in danger of being forgotten.

There are still plenty of cattle ranches around the world—in North America, Australia, and South America, for instance. Cowboys still work hard during spring calving season, during the roundup and branding times, and during the cold winter months at the ranch. Often ranches are operated by the third or fourth generation of the same cowboy family.

But times have changed, too. The cowboy's rope may be nylon, not rawhide. While the horse remains the favorite mode of transportation, a visitor to a modern ranch can also find cowboys carrying out their daily chores on snowmobiles, in trucks, and in helicopters. Computers have entered the front offices of the world's ranches. Ranch lands are subdivided or rented out as cattle prices rise and fall, and owners struggle to make a living.

All over the world, condominiums and modern subdivisions are creeping into the cowboy's workplace. The loud engines of recreational vehicles terrorize the cattle and ruin good grazing land. Visitors on foot and on horseback cause more damage.

So why do cattlemen continue to ranch? Why do cowboys carry on their riding and roping? Many agree that they keep working because of their pride in the cowboy tradition. The cowboy life represents to them honesty, independence, a work ethic, and a respect for the land that they wish to pass down to their children. These truths are not buried in the broken buildings of western ghost towns, nor lost in the romantic visions offered up in films. They are very much alive wherever the cowboy performs his duties, in spite of, and alongside of, the modern world.

Other Books You Might Enjoy

The following titles contain more in-depth discussions of the cowboy and his world. Each book is fully illustrated; titles marked with an asterisk can be found in the adult department of the library and are suitable for older readers or those who wish to study the pictures and captions.

Bellville, Cheryl Walsh. *Rodeo*. Carolrhoda Books, 1985. A Reading Rainbow book, filled with facts and action photographs of the rodeo.

Holling, Holling C. *The Book of Cowboys*. Platt & Munk, 1982. Fictionalized non-fiction. Peter and Barbara Ann go west in this beautifully designed book. Includes glossary.

*Jordan, Teresa. *Cowgirls: Women of the American West, an Oral History*. Anchor Press, Doubleday, 1982. A collection of biographies of cowgirl ranchers and performers, including rodeo stars of this century.

*Sennett, Ted. *Great Hollywood Westerns*. Harry Abrams, 1990. This over-size book is loaded with information and stills from hundreds of westerns. A must for the film buff.

*Siringo, Charles A. *A Texas Cowboy*. Indian Head Books, 1991. A photo-facsimile edition of a cowboy's autobiography originally written in 1885.

*Slatta, Richard W. *Cowboys of the Americas*. Yale University Press, 1990. Tracks the history of the cowboy throughout North and South America.

*Taylor, Lonn and Ingrid Maar. *The American Cowboy*. Library of Congress, 1983. This catalogue is filled with a detailed history and numerous items displayed in a cowboy exhibition.

*Time-Life editors. *The Old West*. Prentice-Hall, 1990. An overview of all facets of Western life, amply illustrated.

*Tyler, Ron. *The Cowboy*. William Morrow, 1979. A lengthy but always interesting history of the cowboy, told with verve and humor.

*Watts, Peter. *A Dictionary of the Old West*. Alfred Knopf, 1977. This reference book provides plenty of information for the trivia fan—and plenty of laughter.

*Weiss, Hillary. *The American Bandanna: Culture on Cloth from George Washington to Elvis*. Chronicle Books, 1990. The entire family can enjoy this history of the bandanna; a number of pages focus on Western motifs.

Index

Picture Credits

Grateful acknowledgment is made to all those who have granted permission to reprint copyrighted material.

Every reasonable effort has been made to locate the copyright holders for these images. The publishers would be pleased to receive information that would allow them to rectify any omissions in future printings.

Page 1: Buffalo Bill Historical Center, Cody, Wyoming, Charles Belden Collection. Page 3: Private collection. Page 4: Glenbow Archives, Calgary, Alberta NA-335-23. Page 5: Author's collection. Page 6: The Rockwell Museum, Corning, New York. Page 8 (upper left): Wyoming State Museum. Pages 8-9: From the collection of Gilcrease Museum, Tulsa. Page 10 (inset): Author's collection. Pages 10-11: Glenbow Archives, Calgary, Alberta NB(H)-16-487. Page 12 (left): Glenbow Archives, Calgary, Alberta NA-101-37. Page 12 (center): Library of Congress. Page 12 (right): Western History Collections, University of Oklahoma Library. Page 13 (bottom left): Glenbow Archives, Calgary, Alberta NA 446-106. Page 13 (center): Adams Memorial Museum, Deadwood, South Dakota. Page 13 (right): National Cowboy Hall of Fame, Oklahoma City. Pages 14-15: Glenbow Archives, Calgary, Alberta NA-2278-1. Page 16 (left): Glenbow Archives, Calgary, Alberta NA-239-27. Pages 16-17: American Heritage Center, University of Wyoming. Page 17 (inset): Author's collection. Pages 18-19: Author's collection. Page 20: Glenbow Archives, Calgary, Alberta NB(H)-16-477. Page 21: Glenbow Archives, Calgary, Alberta NA-3917-62. Page 22: Glenbow Archives, Calgary, Alberta NA 2084-49. Page 23: Glenbow Archives, Calgary, Alberta NA-4461-22. Pages 24-25: The Rockwell Museum, Corning, New York. Page 25: (top right): Glenbow Archives, Calgary, Alberta NA-2084-20. Page 26: Glenbow Archives, Calgary, Alberta NA-446-99. Page 27: Library of Congress. Page 28: Wyoming State Museum. Page 29: Courtesy of John B. Stetson Company. Page 30: Glenbow Archives, Calgary, Alberta NA 3917-63. Page 31: From *The American Bandanna: Culture on Cloth from George Washington to Elvis* by Hillary Weiss © 1990, published by Chronicle Books. Page 32: Glenbow Archives, Calgary, Alberta NA 1483-10.Page 33 (top): Glenbow Archives, Calgary, Alberta NA 118-3. Page 33 (bottom): Courtesy of Don and Barb Merback, Casper, Wyoming. Page 34 (left): Wyoming State Museum. Page 34 (right): Montana Historical Society, Helena. Page 35: Courtesy Levi Strauss Archives. Page 36 (top): Kansas State Historical Society, Topeka, Kansas. Page 36 (bottom): Ribbonhead Ranch House Gallery, Toronto. Page 37 (top): Glenbow Archives, Calgary, Alberta P-4239-70. Page 37 (bottom left): Library of Congress. Page 37 (bottom right): Author's collection. Pages 38-39: Seth. Page 40 (top): Library of Congress. Page 40 (bottom): The Rockwell Museum, Corning, New York. Pages 40-41: Western History Collections, University of Oklahoma Library. Page 42: Author's collection. Page 43 (top right): Glenbow Archives, Calgary, Alberta P-4239-68. Page 43 (bottom left): Glenbow Archives, Calgary, Alberta NB-16-260. Page 43 (bottom right): Library of Congress. Page 44: Wyoming State Museum. Page 45: Glenbow Archives, Calgary, Alberta NB(H)-16-492. Page 46: Denver Public Library, Western History Department. Page 47: The Erwin E. Smith Collection of the Library of Congress on deposit at the Amon Carter Museum. Page 48: Denver Public Library, Western History Department. Page 49: Seth. Page 50: Denver Public Library, Western History Department. Page 51: Glenbow Archives, Calgary, Alberta NA-207-108. Page 52: Glenbow Archives, Calgary, Alberta NB(H)-16-452. Page 53: Western History Collections, University of Oklahoma Library. Page 54: Seth. Page 55 (top): Seth. Page 55 (bottom): Buffalo Bill Historical Center, Cody, Wyoming. Page 56: Denver Public Library, Western History Department. Page 57 (top right): Library of Congress. Page 57 (bottom): Denver Public Library, Western History Department. Page 58: Kansas State Historical Society, Topeka, Kansas. Page 59: Glenbow Archives, Calgary, Alberta NA-782-2. Page 60: Amon Carter Museum, Fort Worth, Texas. Page 61: Kansas State Historical Society, Topeka, Kansas. Page 62 (top left): Kansas State Historical Society, Topeka, Kansas. Page 62 (top right): Oklahoma Historical Society, Archives and Manuscripts Division. Pages 62-63: From the collection of Gilcrease Museum, Tulsa. Page 63 (center): Kansas State Historical Society, Topeka, Kansas. Page 63 (right): Courtesy of Panhandle-Plains Historical Museum, Canyon, Texas. Page 64: Denver Public Library, Western History Department. Page 65: Kansas State Historical Society, Topeka, Kansas. Page 66 (top left): Kansas State Historical Society, Topeka, Kansas. Page 66 (bottom left): Glenbow Archives, Calgary, Alberta NA-4179-22. Page 67 (top right): Lee Moorhouse Collection, University of Oregon. Page 67 (bottom right): Montana Stockgrowers' Association, courtesy of the Montana Historical Society. Page 68 (top left & right): Library of Congress. Page 68 (top center): Denver Public Library, Western History Department. Page 68 (bottom): Library of Congress. Page 69 (top left): Special Collections, University of Nevada-Reno Library. Page 69 (bottom right): Denver Public Library, Western History Department. Page 70 (left): Courtesy Frederic Remington Art Museum, Ogdensburg, New York. Page 70 (center): Montana Historical Society. Page 70 (right): The Rockwell Museum, Corning, New York. Page 71 (top): The Erwin E. Smith Collection of the Library of Congress on deposit at the Amon Carter Museum. Page 71 (bottom): The Rockwell Museum, Corning, New York. Page 72: Museum of Modern Art, Film Stills Archive. Pages 72-73: Author's collection. Page 73 (right): Still from *Divided Loyalties* courtesy of Baton Broadcasting Inc. Page 74 (left): Author's collection. Page 74 (top): *Gunfight at the OK Corral* Copyright © 1993 by Paramount Pictures. All rights reserved. Page 74 (bottom): Library of Congress. Page 75 (top): *Shane* Copyright © 1993 by Paramount Pictures. All rights reserved. Page 75 (inset left): *One-Eyed Jacks* Copyright © 1993 by Paramount Pictures. All rights reserved. Page 75 (inset right): *Unforgiven* © 1992 Warner Brothers. All rights reserved. Courtesy of Warner Brothers. Page 76 (left): The Will Rogers Memorial, Claremore, Oklahoma. Page 76 (inset): Author's collection. Page 77 (left): Roy Rogers Enterprises. Page 77 (right): Seth. Page 77 (inset): Still from *High Noon* courtesy of Republic Pictures Corporation. Pages 78-79 (top): Seth. Page 79 (top right & bottom left): © John R. Hamilton. Page 80 (left): Courtesy of Andy McLean. Page 80 (center): Courtesy of Dan Yamasaki. Page 81 (center): Courtesy of the Eaton Archives. Page 82 (left): Glenbow Archives, Calgary, Alberta NA-2771-1. Page 82 (right): Denver Public Library, Western History Department. Page 83 (top): "Powder River" Jack and Kittie Lee at Calgary Stampede, Glenbow Archives, Calgary, Alberta NA-446-120. Page 83 (bottom): Author's collection. Page 84 (top): © Dargaud Editeur Paris 1968 by Goscinny & Morris. Page 84 (bottom): Collection of Michael Solomon. Page 85 (top): Heather Hafleigh, Western Folklife Center, Elko, Nevada. Page 85 (bottom): Glenbow Archives, Calgary, Alberta NA-2573-1. Page 86 (top left to right): Glenbow Archives, Calgary, Alberta NA-335-65, NB(H)-16-271, NA-5093-686. Page 86 (center): Glenbow Archives, Calgary, Alberta NB(H)-16-276. Page 87: Glenbow Archives, Calgary, Alberta NA-604-1A. Page 88: © Mike Drew, reprinted with permission of TG Magazine, 119 Collier Street, Barrie, Ontario L4M 1H5. Page 89 (top left): Glenbow Archives, Calgary, Alberta NA- 446-107. Page 89 (top center & right): Courtesy of Ryan Byrne. Page 89 (middle & bottom left): Glenbow Archives, Calgary, Alberta NA-335-21, 79.26.3894. Page 89 (bottom): Western History Collections, University of Oklahoma Library. Pages 90-91: © Mike Drew, Calgary. Pages 92-93: © Sig Galk, Vancouver.